# WordPress Security for Webmaster 2017

How to Stop Hackers Breaking into Your Website

Dr. Andy Williams

Released: 4th September 2017

GW00728799

# DISCLAIMER AND TERMS OF USE AGREEMENT

The author and publisher of this eBook and the accompanying materials have used their best efforts in preparing this eBook. The author and publisher make no representation or warranties with respect to the accuracy, applicability, fitness, or completeness of the contents of this eBook. The information contained in this eBook is strictly for educational purposes. Therefore, if you wish to apply ideas contained in this eBook, you are taking full responsibility for your actions.

The author and publisher disclaim any warranties (express or implied), merchantability, or fitness for any particular purpose. The author and publisher shall in no event be held liable to any party for any direct, indirect, punitive, special, incidental or other consequential damages arising directly or indirectly from any use of this material, which is provided "as is", and without warranties.

The author and publisher don't warrant the performance, effectiveness or applicability of any sites listed or linked to in this eBook.

All links are for information purposes only and are not warranted for content, accuracy or any other implied or explicit purpose.

The author and publisher of this book are not in any way associated with Google.

# Contents

# Who Am I & Why Should You Listen to Me?

My name is Andy Williams, and I'm a qualified and experienced teacher. In 2001, I gave up teaching in schools. Till then I'd been a science teacher working with students from 11 to 18 years of age. But I needed a new challenge, and most of all, I wanted to spend more time with my family.

Since then my work has been to study the search engines and build websites for profit. It's been a long journey but I've not traveled it alone. A large number of people joined me by reading my free weekly newsletter. I still publish it, over at ezSEONews.com. My newsletter covers a wide range of topics, relevant to webmasters in particular. Webmasters are the people who own and build their own website(s). You can also sign up to receive my free newsletter if it interests you.

In the early days, websites were hand-built using special code called Hyper Text Markup Language (HTML). To create good-looking websites back then, you had to be something of a geek. Then, special tools came onto the market to reduce the learning curve associated with building websites in HTML. Two of the more popular ones were Macromedia Dreamweaver (now owned by Adobe), and Microsoft Front Page (discontinued in 2006). The problem with these web development tools is that they were expensive.

In May 2003, Matt Mullenweg & Mike Little, released a new tool that would change the face of website building forever. They called it WordPress.

I have to admit, I was a little reluctant to give up my copy of Dreamweaver at first. But in 2004, I began to experiment with the WordPress platform. It was a time when WordPress was just starting to get interesting. This was thanks to the introduction of something we now know as "plugins".

Fast-forward to today and WordPress is now the site-building tool of choice. It's popular with professionals and enthusiasts alike. Home-based businesses run by moms & dads love it, as do school kids running blogs about their favorite bands. Today, even large corporations use WordPress, and just about everyone else who builds websites.

WordPress is extremely powerful, flexible, and produces very professional looking websites and blogs. It's pretty easy to use too, but best of all is that it's 100% free.

The other advantage of WordPress is that the code is freely available to anyone who needs it. This same advantage, though, is also its biggest security threat. The open nature of the code means developers can create exciting new plugins and themes to extend the functionality. Alas, it also means hackers can find security holes in the code and use them to gain illegal access to WordPress websites.

A lot of the discussion on website security can get overly technical. Even so, the average webmaster needs to be able to protect and secure their website. That means there should be no technical barriers to stop the average user. It's why we need these things written in plain and simple English.

This is where I come in.

I have years of experience teaching technical stuff in an easy to understand manner. I'm going to take you by the hand and guide you — one easy step at a time — as you secure your own website(s) against hackers.

My book is a step-by-step, visual guide to website security. I've included screenshots where I think they can help, so you just need to follow along at your own pace. In no time at all, your website will be just about hack-proof.

Excited?

OK, let's get on with it.

# How to Use This Book

I wrote this book for anyone who runs a WordPress website. I won't assume you have any technical knowledge at all. You don't have to worry about steep learning curves or technical skill requirements. There aren't any.

What you have here is a hands-on tutorial. To get the most out of it, I recommend you sit at your computer and follow the steps outlined in these pages. Whenever I do something on my demo site, you do the same on your own site. Don't be afraid to make mistakes as they can easily be undone.

There are two main sections in the book.

The first section looks at the various ways hackers can gain access to your site and how you can STOP them. I also provide detailed instructions on ways to plug these security holes. Don't worry; you don't need to do anything at this point, not if you don't want to.

The second part of the book covers a comprehensive security plugin. This plugin secures your site using a simple point-and-click interface. You'll learn about website security in the very first section of the book. You then just follow my lead as we set up the plugin to secure your site against hackers.

By the end of this book, you'll have a solid understanding of WordPress security. You'll also know the measures to take to secure your own website(s).

I have good news for anyone who likes to learn via audio-visual. You should find my companion WordPress Security video course very interesting. There are around 2.5 hours of video tuition and a Q&A section where you can ask me questions. I host this course on the Udemy platform, and I've created a special discount link for readers of this book.

Using the link below, you can get the WordPress Security course for just $10:

http://ezseonews.com/securebook

A note about UK v US English

There're some differences between UK and US English. While I strive to be consistent, some errors may occasionally slip into my writing. It's probably because I spend a lot of time corresponding with people in the UK and the US. The line can blur. Examples of this include spelling of words like optimise (UK) v optimize (US).

The thing I get the most complaints about is with collective nouns. Collective nouns refer to a group of individuals, e.g. Google. In the US, collective nouns are singular, so Google IS a search engine. However, in the UK, collective nouns are usually plural, so Google ARE a search engine.

There are other differences as well. Please bear this in mind if you find random inconsistencies within the book. If you do, I hope any of these minor details won't detract from the value you get from these pages.

**About typos:**

Occasional typos can slip the net even in costly, professional publications. I hope you don't come across any in this book, but you may do. If you do find any typos, I'd be very grateful if you could let me know so that I can fix it/them. You can send me a message using this email address:

typos@ezseonews.com

# SECTION 1 - About Security & Hacking

The first section of the book outlines the main ways a hacker will try to gain access to your site. It also looks at how you can prevent these things from happening.

# Chapter 1 - Introduction

Estimates from 2016, suggest that only 44% of website traffic was genuine, human visitors. Bots, hacking tools, scrapers, and spammers made up the other 56%.

It's thought that around 30,000+ websites get hacked every single day. So online security has to be the main concern for anyone who runs a website, no matter how small their project is.

Securi (a top internet security service) releases a quarterly report on hacking attempts. Their data from the third quarter of 2016 was alarming to say the least. It suggested that WordPress made up 74% of all infected websites.

Hackers hack websites for a variety of purposes. Some will want to redirect your traffic. Hackers also attempt to steal customer details, delete files, or change your login details to lock you out. Some will send spam emails to millions of people, SEO for the hacker's site, and other, more sinister reasons.

Don't think that your small, insignificant site is safe from hackers—it's not. To a hacker, a site is a site, and they'll attack it if it serves their purpose. They use computer software to auto-scan millions of websites for vulnerabilities. Once found, they'll attack any soft targets they come across. There is no softer target than a newly setup WordPress website run from a bedroom.

There are good reasons to worry about your website security. Despite the scare, I don't want you to avoid WordPress thinking it's an insecure platform. It isn't. WordPress is actually very secure. When the WordPress security team find a security hole they usually plug it fast. They then automatically push the update out to all WordPress installs.

The real security issues derive from the folks who run the websites. They often don't have the knowledge to make the best informed decisions. They don't know enough about content, the plugins they use, or the themes they install.

**This book has two aims:**

1. I want to give you the knowledge you need so you can understand where the main threats come from. With this knowledge, you'll understand how your administrative actions can affect the security of your website. Your new understanding then gives you the power to stop hackers.

2. I want to give you a step-by-step solution to make your website as hackproof as possible. We'll install an excellent WordPress plugin and go through the entire setup process. For your part, just follow along on your own site as I secure one of my own.

If you're not technically minded, don't worry. This book assumes no technical ability and no programming skills.

# Chapter 2 – Why Do Hackers Hack

I guess you want something a little more than *because they can*, right?

Unfortunately, this is the reason for a large number of hacking attempts these days. Hackers often leave behind a calling card to show how clever they are. It's often in the form of a banner, announcing their uninvited presence on your site. It's a kind of virtual ego trip.

Hackers can cause all kinds of damage on your site.

They might delete your content just for laughs. Others "silently" insert malicious code into a site to carry out some dastardly plan. The webmaster doesn't usually get any visual clues to show that someone has compromised their beloved site.

Hacking causes chaos to the site owner and is often time-consuming and expensive to clean up. Some of the more common reasons why hacker's hack include:

1.  To break into a popular site to stage some kind of protest.

2.  To post banners or extremist messages to support their cause.

3.  To insert malware that auto-downloads to the computers of those who visit the pages. This malware can cause all kinds of chaos. They can use it to steal personal data (like credit card details) from the computers it infects.

4.  To send huge volumes of spam emails from your domain. This action is likely to get your site closed down by your web host. It's not your fault that millions upon millions of spammy emails leave your server over a short space of time. Despite this, your site cannot be live until you resolve the problem.

5.  To gain a competitive advantage. They may embed links into your pages for their SEO purposes. They might also do it to destroy the SEO of the target site so that it drops out of Google's search engine results pages (SERPs).

The bad news is that no amount of security on any site can guarantee it'll be 100% hacker proof. It all depends on the motivation and resources of the hackers involved. You may have seen recent news reports on some very major hacks.

For example, in September 2016, Yahoo revealed that it was the victim of a major hack attack. In that case, hackers breached at least 500 million user accounts. This followed the one billion Yahoo accounts breached in August 2013.

You may have also seen an increase in something called ransomware attacks around the world in 2017.

Those of you in the US will be aware of the controversy over the recent presidential elections. Over there you have the ongoing investigations about possible electoral manipulation from outside the country.

The good news is that once you've finished this book, you'll be a lot safer than most other WordPress websites. The type of hacker that's usually responsible for hacking an average website is not going to have the time, patience, or resources to break into yours. Remember, most of these guys look for "soft targets".

So there are two sections to this book. You can treat the first one as information-only if you like. I show you some manual procedures for securing against hackers in this section. However, it's not necessary for you to do anything as you read the first part. The second section covers a WordPress plugin that secures against all the important threats. This is where I show you the step-by-step instructions on how to install it and set it up to secure your site.

# Chapter 3 - WordPress Really Is Secure But?

WordPress has a bad reputation when it comes to security, but that reputation is wrong. It's true; WordPress websites do tend to get hacked a lot. Remember, 74% of all hacked websites run on WordPress. Still, these hacks are usually because of the WordPress webmaster and not the WordPress core code.

WordPress is open source. That means the programming code behind it is free for anyone to look at and modify if they so wish. They created WordPress this way so that third-party developers could extend its features. That meant anyone could create and distribute new WordPress themes and plugins.

The freedom to offer WordPress enhancements is enough to start alarm bells ringing. Imagine a hacker who wanted to infiltrate a lot of websites. What better way than to develop a really useful plugin, or a cool theme, and offer them for free?  Can you see the problem?

Plugins and themes represent one of the top three ways to hack a WordPress website. If the plugin or theme is not in itself malicious, it could still have vulnerabilities in its code. Any weaknesses can provide a doorway to hackers.

The good news is that WordPress runs "repositories" for themes and plugins. WordPress.org carefully vets any plugin or theme included in these repositories. This safeguard is to ensure they don't contain any vulnerabilities or malicious code. So they key here is to simply choose plugins and themes from authorized sources. Just by doing this you already take a giant step to secure your site against hackers.

So, plugins & themes are one of the top three ways for hackers to hack WordPress websites and blogs. Maybe you can guess the other two?

- Weak usernames and passwords
- Not keeping software up to date

Weak usernames and passwords are a common route to a hack. They're a hassle though, right? After all, we have so many usernames and passwords to remember these days. This includes things like bank details, website logins, utility bill sites, and online shopping stores, etc. It's the reason why a lot of people use the same username and/or password for multiple site logins.

Be warned!

If a hacker gets access to just one of your accounts, they can usually gain access to a lot more by using the same login details.

Think about your own passwords.

Do you have them written down in a little book somewhere?  What if you lose that book or someone steals it?  Do you use the same password for multiple online accounts? Is it a "secure" password? It's a good question, bearing in mind that automated software tools can try hundreds of password combinations a second?

We'll go over the dos and don'ts of passwords later in the book.

Not updating software is another very common problem. Software includes things like themes, plugins, and WordPress core files. When the WordPress team find vulnerabilities, they're usually quick to plugs them. If you keep WordPress up to date, hackers cannot use those vulnerabilities to gain access. If you don't keep it up to date, hackers have an easy way into your site.

What makes things even easier for hackers is that WordPress can show them exactly what version you're using. All they have to do then is look up vulnerabilities in that particular version and use them to hack your site.

This all sounds really bad, doesn't it? Don't panic!

There's one thing these three major security issues have in common that gives you the upper hand:

THE USER CAUSES THE PROBLEMS, NOT WORDPRESS.

As the webmaster, it's what you do (or don't do) to your site that makes it secure or insecure. I say again, WordPress is actually very secure.

There's a team of 25 experts (researchers and developers) who continually work to make WordPress even more secure. Since version 3.7, automated updates fix all security issues routinely, without you having to lift a finger.

# Chapter 4 - Learning What Needs to Be Secured

This chapter takes you through the main security threats. It's where I offer you some advice on what you should be doing to secure your site. In some cases, you can go ahead and make changes as you read through the chapter. In most instances, though, I'll tell you not to worry about doing anything right away. This is because the security plugin we install and configure in the second part of the book will do it all for you.

I've broken the chapter down into "threats." Each "threat" covers a security issue you should know about. Before we start to look at these threats, let's consider the only way to protect your site 100%.

## Back Up Your Website

The only real way to make your website safe is to back it up. Whatever happens after that, at least you'll always have the files saved to replicate the site again. Even if it means starting over, it's still better than losing everything.

With traditional HTML-based websites, backing up is a simple process. You just copy the files on your hosting server to your own computer (download), and that's your full backup. WordPress is a little more complicated, though.

A WordPress website consists of two main parts:

1. The files. This includes the WordPress core files, plugins, themes, and uploaded files like images, and settings.

2. The Database, which stores all your website content.

For a full WordPress website, you need to back up the files AND the database.

There are a lot of tools and plugins available to help you backup your WordPress website. It's important to check what they back up-exactly.

Some only do partial backups like the database. The more useful ones will backup both the database and all the files.

You may think that the only way to do a proper backup is to do a full one. First, you need to be aware of the file size of these backups.

The database-only backups are typically 1-5 MB in size. You can even have these emailed to you.

Full backups can be gigabytes (GB) in size, and they use a lot of server resources to process. Clearly you cannot receive these by email.

The solution is to use a plugin like UpdraftPlus. There's a free version which is more than adequate for most users. The premium version is great for anyone who needs more power and options.

UpdraftPlus' free version can automatically backup your site to a remote storage location on a predefined schedule. It includes popular online storage like Dropbox, Google Drive, and Amazon S3, to name a few. If anything should happen to your hosting server, you have offsite backups to fall back on.

To find out more about Updraft, please see:

http://ezseonews.com/updraft

## Installing & Setting up UpdraftPlus

As with most trusted plugins, you can find it in the WordPress repository. You just log in to your WordPress Dashboard and go to "install a new plugin."

Search for "updraft".

As I write this book, you can see the plugin is actively in use by 1+ million websites. It was also updated fairly recently. Both of these metrics provide you with clues to show it's a trusted and actively updated plugin (something you should always look out for).

Install and activate Updraft.

Once active, you'll find a new menu under the **Settings** menu, called **UpdraftPlus Backups**.

Clicking on it takes you to a screen showing the current status:

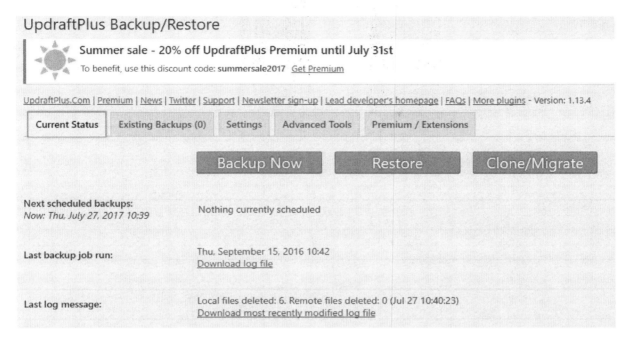

**UpdraftPlus Backup/Restore**

Summer sale - 20% off UpdraftPlus Premium until July 31st
To benefit, use this discount code: summersale2017 Get Premium

UpdraftPlus.Com | Premium | News | Twitter | Support | Newsletter sign-up | Lead developer's homepage | FAQs | More plugins - Version: 1.13.4

| Current Status | Existing Backups (0) | Settings | Advanced Tools | Premium / Extensions |

Backup Now    Restore    Clone/Migrate

**Next scheduled backups:**
Now: Thu, July 27, 2017 10:39

Nothing currently scheduled

**Last backup job run:**

Thu, September 15, 2016 10:42
Download log file

**Last log message:**

Local files deleted: 6. Remote files deleted: 0 (Jul 27 10:40:23)
Download most recently modified log file

In your case, there won't be any backups yet.

I recommend the first thing you do is click the Backup Now button.

You need to choose what to include in your backup, so choose database and files. You'll notice the disabled box referring to remote storage.

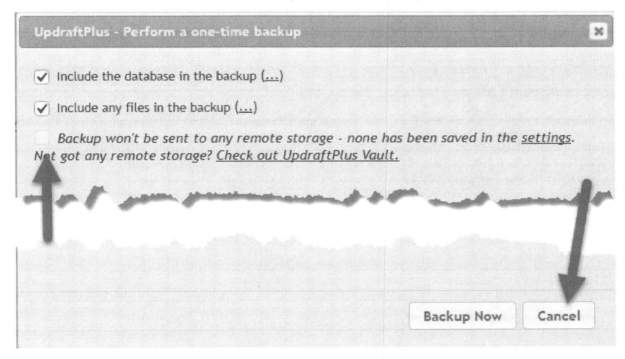

**UpdraftPlus - Perform a one-time backup**

☑ Include the database in the backup (...)

☑ Include any files in the backup (...)

☐ Backup won't be sent to any remote storage - none has been saved in the settings. Not got any remote storage? Check out UpdraftPlus Vault.

Backup Now    Cancel

Since we haven't set up remote storage yet, it isn't an option. The program is currently set to store the backup directly on your web server.

However, a backup is not much use if we store it on a hacked server. This is why we really need to setup some off-site storage.

OK, now cancel the backup and click on the **Settings** tab.

At the top of this screen, you can choose the frequency of automated backups.

The frequency you choose will depend on how often you update your site. If you don't update the site at all, then leave both database and file backups as monthly.

If you update weekly, set the database to weekly but leave the files as monthly.

If you update on a daily basis, set the database frequency to at least daily. The file backup frequency is up to you. But remember, it takes more server resources to back up the files. They're also a lot bigger in size, and therefore use more bandwidth when uploading to your off-site storage.

Personally, I leave files as monthly for all my sites and then adjust the database, depending on how frequently I update the site.

When you set the frequency, you can also choose how many backups to keep. The only real concern here is how much space you have on your remote storage. I would recommend you always have a minimum of at least three months of backups. Therefore, if backups are monthly, keep 3. If they're weekly, keep 12.

You can now choose the remote storage option.

Click your chosen remote storage to select it, and then scroll to the bottom of the page to save the changes. I've chosen Dropbox for mine.

During the process of setting up a storage option, you'll have to authorize UpdraftPlus to log into the chosen site. The note below is for Dropbox:

| Authenticate with Dropbox: | After you have saved your settings (by clicking 'Save Changes' below), then come back here once and click this link to complete authentication with Dropbox. |
| --- | --- |

Once you've saved the settings you need to click the link and sign into Dropbox to complete the authorization.

When done, you can continue to scroll down the settings of this plugin. This is where you choose which files to backup, and those to exclude—if any:

There's also a useful option to have an email report sent with the backup details.

Now click the **save** button at the bottom of the screen. That's all there is to it.

Over on the current status tab, you should now have a **"Next Scheduled Backups"** date. You're free to manually create one now, as well as clicking the **Backup Now** button. You can now see the option to: **Send this backup to remote storage**:

**UpdraftPlus – Perform a one-time backup**

☑ Include the database in the backup (....)

☑ Include any files in the backup (....)

☑ Send this backup to remote storage

With backups done, you now have everything you need to restore your site to its present glory in any eventuality. It's effectively 100% secure already.

With the site backed up, let's now learn of the threats to your website security.

# Threat 1 - Passwords

Earlier in this book, we identified passwords as one of the weakest links in WordPress security.

If you have a strong password, then you have a strong foundation on which to build other security measures. So, what forms a strong password?

There are a few considerations when deciding on a strong password. It should include all the following:

- A random collection of characters
- Include numbers
- Include upper and lower case
- Include special characters

When it comes to passwords, the longer they are the better.

When they released WordPress 4.3, they introduced strong passwords by default. There is also a tool inside the WordPress Dashboard to generate super secure passwords if you need one. You can find it in your user profile:

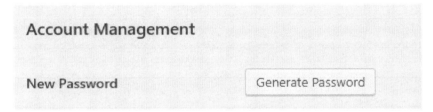

To generate a secure password, click the **Generate Password** button and WordPress will create one for you:

If you look at the password, you can see it meets the criteria I specified at the start. It's random, includes numbers, upper and lower case and special characters (#, & and %). It's also a lot longer (24 characters) than the passwords most people make up themselves.

The tool will also give you an idea of how strong your password is. Type it into the box and make sure your password reads **Strong** under the data input field.

I know most people's objection to this type of password.

It's impossible to remember.

That's correct, but there are some great tools out there. These tools not only remember your passwords, they can auto-fill them for you as well. I personally use a tool called Roboform and can highly recommend it. Roboform remembers all my secure passwords (and I have hundreds), and it automatically fills them in for me whenever I visit a website.

**NOTE:** If you're just installing WordPress, you won't have access to the Dashboard yet, or the password generator tool. Never mind. Do a Google search for **secure password generator** instead. You'll find a few tools which can create these strong, random passwords for you. Lastpass is another popular password manager that provides a free secure password generator. You can get it here:

https://lastpass.com/generatepassword.php

Here are your options with this tool:

Password Length:

24

Password Formula:

⦿ Allow All Character Types

○ Make Pronounceable?

☑ A-Z  ☑ a-z  ☑ 0-9  ☑ !$%@#

5   Minimum Numeric Characters:

☐ Avoid Ambiguous Characters

You can choose a 24 character password as WordPress suggests, plus all the other criteria. Here is a sample password generated with that tool:

R!%x7Lq021k5LCF^9SJO1dEc

Select Password

Generate

You can also find free tools online that will check how secure a password is. Here's one example:

That's a strong password!

Before you move on in the book, make sure you update your password if necessary to make it strong and long.

Again, if you need software to remember passwords, I highly recommend Roboform:

http://ezseonews.com/roboform

## Threat 2 - WordPress Usernames

Usernames and passwords go together like peanut butter and jelly (that's jam in the UK). They're very important as a hacker needs both to log into a website.

Unfortunately, when WordPress installs, it uses the default username **admin. M**ost newbies to WordPress don't bother to change it, but they should. By not changing it, you give hackers half of what they need to log into your site!

If you already have your site installed and DID use **admin** as your username, don't panic. When we install the security plugin later, we'll check this and change it if necessary.

When you install WordPress, you can choose your own, unique username, and you already know what to do about the password.

Choose a username that is:

- Not easy to guess
- Not **admin**

When I choose a new username, I use the same criteria as for passwords, though maybe only 12-15 characters in length.

# Threat 3 – Signing In

When you log into your website, make sure you check the address bar at the top of your browser BEFORE you log in.

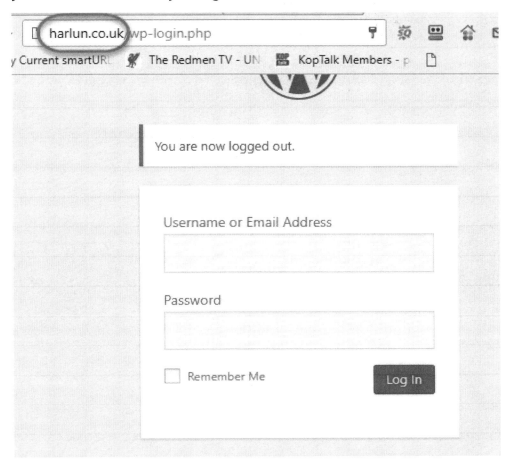

Here I am at one of my sites and I can see the login form. However, get used to glancing up at the domain in the address bar before you log in. Make absolutely sure it's YOUR domain.

If a hacker is able to inject code into your web site, they can setup a redirect. That means as you try to log in, you're taken to a completely different domain. This is one the hacker owns, and it'll have a dummy login form. You think you're logging into your own site, but you're not. Then, as you enter your username and password, you've just given the hacker your login details.

## Threat 4 - PHP Error Reporting

PHP is a widely used open-source programming language. It's great for most kinds of web development, so it's no surprise to learn that WordPress is coded in PHP.

Besides the WordPress core files, WordPress themes and plugins also add PHP code to your website. As with any kind of programming, bugs in the code can cause problems. WordPress will tell you when an error occurs, as well as the line of code that caused it. That's great for developers. Alas, hackers can also use these error messages to gain more information about your web server.

Fortunately, there's a way to stop WordPress issuing these error reports, therefore disabling PHP error reporting.

The security plugin we install later in the book doesn't take care of this for you. If you want to disable error reporting, here's how you do it.

You need to add a special line of code to your wp-config.php file. You can find this file in the root folder of your domain.

The simple line of code is as follows: **error_reporting(0);**

Place the code right after the opening **<?php** tag and above all the other code in the file as per the image:

If you ever need to see the error messages in the future, simply come in and remove this line of code while you're working on your site. You can either delete it or comment it out using the format below:

**/* error_reporting(0); */**

The /* at the start and the */ at the end stops any commands inside from being read. When you've finished the work on your site, you can remove the comment markers to once again disable PHP error reporting.

# Threat 5 – File Editor

The file editor inside your WordPress Dashboard is invaluable. It gives you — or any other admin user logged into your account — access to theme and plugin files.

To edit theme files, go to the **Appearance** menu and select **Editor**.

To edit plugin files, go to the **Plugins** menu and select **Editor**.

The problem we have is that anyone with access to these files can "inject" malicious code into your website. So if the logged in user is a hacker, the consequences can be catastrophic.

The good news is you can disable these editors by adding a single line of code to your wp-config.php file.

I'm going to show you how to do this manually, BUT, this is for information only. The plugin we install in the second part of this book will do the work for you.

For those who want to do this manually now, here's how it works.

This wp-config.php file is in the root folder of your website. You can gain access to it by using FTP or the File Manager inside cPanel.

Here's the wp-config.php file for one of my test sites:

```php
<?php
/**
 * The base configuration for WordPress
 *
 * The wp-config.php creation script uses this file during the
 * installation. You don't have to use the web site, you can
 * copy this file to "wp-config.php" and fill in the values.
 *
 * This file contains the following configurations:
 *
 * * MySQL settings
 * * Secret keys
 * * Database table prefix
 * * ABSPATH
 *
 * @link https://codex.wordpress.org/Editing_wp-config.php
 *
 * @package WordPress
 */

// ** MySQL settings - You can get this info from your web host ** //
/** The name of the database for WordPress */
```

I've drawn an arrow at the point where I'm going to insert the line of code.

Position your cursor in the blank line right before the line that starts:

// ** MySQL settings - ...

In this line, insert the following code:

define('DISALLOW_FILE_EDIT', true);

When you've done that, save your wp-config.php file and make sure it overwrites the older version.

Now log in to your WordPress Dashboard. You'll no longer see the options to use the editor. Here's how the Appearance menu looks now:

*(Ignore the bottom four items in the sub-menu. My own personal theme and plugins have added these to my list).*

Here's the Plugins menu:

# Threat 6 – Control the Content Published on Your Site

This is common sense, I know. It's still vital to realize how security issues can result from the stuff you publish.

When you create a page or post in WordPress, you have an option to embed code into that page or post. For example, it could be YouTube video code, JavaScript, or something else.

The only reason you add code to your pages is to add some form of functionality or feature. If you're non-technical, then you may not understand the code, and that's okay. But what is vitally important is that you trust the source. Remember, malicious code gives hackers a back door into your website or web server.

The "common sense" rules that apply here are:

1. Don't embed any code into a post or a page unless you trust the source 100%, or know the code is safe.

For example, you know you can embed a YouTube video into your page, as Google owns YouTube. They are a trusted source.

If you're an affiliate marketer and you want to embed some affiliate code given to you by Amazon, then that is fine too. Amazon is another trusted source.

But if you join an unknown affiliate scheme and they ask you to embed code into your pages, get the code checked out. Only put it into your posts if you trust the person or company that gave it to you 100%.

2. Be careful if you allow other people to publish content on your site. I suggest you manually approve all new submissions before you publish them. The quick way to check the content is to switch over to the **Text** tab of the WordPress editor so you can see if there's any code in the article. Don't publish anything that contains code you were unaware of or are uncertain about.

3. If you allow visitors to leave comments, DON'T auto-approve them. Even comments can have code embedded into them. It's safer to check comments manually first and only approve them when you're sure.

**IMPORTANT**: There is an option in WordPress that allows you to auto-approve comments from visitors that have had at least one comment approved previously.

| Before a comment appears | ☐ Comment must be manually approved |
|---|---|
| | ☑ Comment author must have a previously approved comment |

Don't enable it.

This was the way a lot of WordPress sites got hacked in the past. A hacker would submit a good comment to get it approved manually. They'd then use their new "auto-approved" status to add comments with code embedded. It's much safer to moderate ALL comments manually.

We'll revisit comment security later in the book.

# Threat 7 - New Users

A WordPress website can have more than one user.

A "user" in this context means anyone who can log in to the WordPress Dashboard. It has nothing to do with being a "visitor." A visitor is anyone who turns up to view your website in their web browser.

Some sites allow visitors to register as users, giving them login details to access the Dashboard. What they can do after they register depends on the privileges you give them. At the one end, users can simply edit their own profile. At the other end, users can administer (control and manage) the entire site. It's important that you give any additional users the right privileges.

At this point, you might wonder why a webmaster would allow visitors to become users. Here are some of the most popular reasons:

- To allow guest bloggers on the site. That is, allow your visitors to create posts (fresh content) on your site. This is usually in return for a link they include somewhere in the article. Unless you trust them and know exactly what you're doing, I don't recommend having guest bloggers post on your website. They pose a security problem, as well as an SEO headache.

- To create a membership site. If you decide you want to create a membership site, I recommend you use the **Wishlist Member** WordPress plugin. The plugin adds extra layers of security and gives you a lot more options for configuring and setting up your site. If you're interested in learning more, I have a course on building a membership site with **Wishlist Member**. There's a link to all my video courses at the end of this book.

- To create a mailing list of "subscribers". The best way to create a mailing list is to use proper third party tools. One of the best ones for mailing lists and autoresponders is Aweber – http://ezseo.aweber.com. Companies like Aweber shield you from a lot of potential security (and hosting) issues. Security and hosting hassles can arise when you try to set this type of thing up on your own domain.

For safety reasons, my advice is to NOT let unknown visitors register as users. There's a setting in the WordPress Dashboard you need to check.

## Anyone can register

In the General Settings, make sure **Anyone can register** is unchecked like this:

| Membership | ☐ Anyone can register |
|---|---|

This should be off (unchecked) by default. It will only show as active if you, or someone else, checked it at some point.

If you choose to enable this option, I highly recommend you set the default role to "Subscriber". That'll give new users basic access without the opportunity to cause much damage. You can then change these roles on a one by one basis if you want to elevate a user's privileges at any point.

The options you have for roles are as follows:

- Subscriber: can manage their own profile.
- Contributor: can write guest posts but not publish them (best option).
- Author: can write and publish their posts.
- Editor: Can write, publish and manage ALL posts.
- Administrator: full access to the site and all administrative screens.
- Super Admin: a network administrator when using networked WordPress (not an option with the regular version of WordPress).

If you decide to allow visitors to register as users, only give them the privileges they need and no more. This is the most important piece of advice I can give you, so please take heed.

## Usernames & Passwords

We looked at usernames and passwords earlier in the book, and how important they are to keep your site safe. The same is true for ALL users on your site. If you have multiple users, your site is only as secure as its weakest link.

When you allow other users to register, you need to make sure they all use very secure usernames and passwords.

Although WordPress automatically generates a secure password for each new user, they can still edit their profile. That means they can also change their password. Don't ever let users change their secure password for an insecure one.

# Threat 8 - Widgets & Code

Earlier in the book we looked at why you need to control the content of your site and the common sense rules surrounding published content. We saw code as one potential problem. I want to revisit code here because widgets can pose a threat.

For example, the text widget can contain any text you like, including code. Here is a text widget on one of my websites:

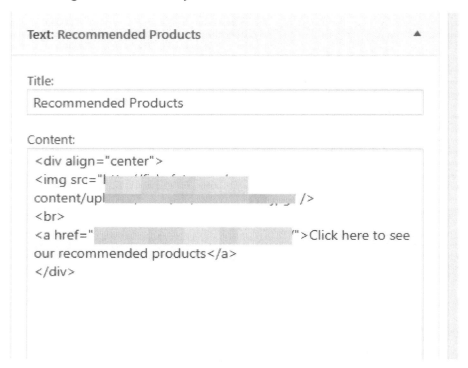

The code above is HTML and displays some recommended products in the sidebar. I understand the code and know it's safe to use, so it's fine. But what if you don't understand what the code does or what it means?

Let's recap the common sense rules again:

- Only put code into your posts, pages and widgets if you absolutely trust the source and know the code is trustworthy.

- Only install widgets (installed as plugins) if you trust the source of the plugin 100%.

- Plugins and themes you get from the official WordPress repositories should be safe. For your part, you still need to update them regularly in case any vulnerability issues need fixing. Keeping themes and plugins up to date minimizes the risk from hackers.

- If you buy themes or plugins from other websites, is the source trustworthy?

Do your due diligence on Google and read any reviews. Are there any customer comments to concern you?

# Embedding Code in a Post or Page

I want to show you a bit of code to highlight a potential issue. You will see how easy it is to spot once you know what to look for.

Highlight and copy the HTML below, then paste it into the code for your Web site

```
<a target="_blank" href="https://www.amazon.com/gp/product/B01MQD63WX/ref=as_li_tl?
ie=UTF8&camp=1789&creative=9325&creativeASIN=B01MQD63WX&linkCode=as2&tag=teach
er1stop-20&linkId=5b3e5b494373ce07f5fb915f19e5f4f9">2016 Premium High Performance
RCA Galileo Pro 11.5" 32GB Touchscreen Tablet Computer with Keyboard Case Quad-Core
1.3Ghz Processor 1G Memory 32GB HDD Webcam Wifi Bluetooth Android 6.0-Black</a><img
src="//ir-na.amazon-adsystem.com/e/ir?t=teacher1stop-20&l=am2&o=1&a=B01MQD63WX"
width="1" height="1" border="0" alt="" style="border:none !important; margin:0px !important;"
/>
```

This code is from Amazon and is safe.

What I want you to look out for are URLs that don't belong to your site. The code above has two. If you know any HTML, you'll know that the first mention of Amazon.com is the URL for a text link. The second is an image displayed with the advert. This is all fine because we understand the code.

But what if you get some code you don't understand.

Take this example:

Copy Ad Code

```
<script type="text/javascript">amazon_ad_tag ="santschri-21"; amazon_ad_width ="120";
amazon_ad_height ="600"; </script><script src="http://ir-uk.amazon-adsystem.com/s/ads.js">
</script>
```

OK, the URL is to amazon-adsystem.com. I assume it's an Amazon controlled domain, so is safe. If you're unsure, you can check with a quick search on Google. Just search Google for the domain and see what comes back. In this case, it's a legitimate domain used by Amazon to serve ads. You need to verify any suspicious or unfamiliar URLs found in the code you add to your posts or pages.

**IMPORTANT:** That URL actually calls some JavaScript (JS) code (ads.js). You don't get to see the actual JS code that'll be running on your site. It could be anything, and do pretty much what it wants on your page(s). Can you see why you need to trust the code you add 100%?

# Threat 9 - Plugins

Plugins are basically pieces of code that add new features to your WordPress site.

Since code can control pretty much every aspect of a site, including malicious things, you need to be sure you can trust the plugins you use.

Although much of this is also common sense, here are a few helpful tips:

- Only install plugins from trusted sources. The WordPress repository is the main trusted source. Sometimes, you may want to buy something that isn't in there. In these cases, do your due diligence and check out reviews and customer comments on those plugins.

- Developers who create free plugins come in two forms. There are the good guys who are happy to help and want to create a useful, free plugin with no strings attached. Then there are those who want to profit from their free plugin. There are a number of ways to do this. The most common method is to give away a free trial version. They hope you'll upgrade to a paid version with more features and functions after the trial period. These can be fine but again, do your due diligence.

  The type of plugin to be wary of are those which include code that doesn't directly contribute to the functionality you're trying to gain. For example, a mortgage calculator that adds a link back to the lender's website. In this case you want the functionality of the calculator. Yet the bank has included other, unrelated code, to that function. In this case, it's a link pointing back to their website. My advice is to avoid this type of plugin at all costs.

- Always keep plugins up to date. Be wary of those that have no known updates, or have not had an update in a very long time. There are also legitimate plugins that just don't get updates. For example, they use secure code and the author doesn't want to add new features. These are fine. If there's a plugin you want, but it's been a while since its last update, check it out on Google. Use a search term like "plugin name + security" to see if there are any reported issues.

- If you deactivate a plugin, uninstall it altogether. Even inactive plugins CAN cause security problems if they contain vulnerable code.

## Threat 10 - Themes

Themes, like plugins, add code to your website.

The same kind of common sense measures we talked about for plugins also apply to themes. Here are some guidelines.

- The WordPress theme repository is a safe place to get themes. Many people still want to look further afield to find the best themes for their website. Be careful where you get yours from. Again, do a search on Google for the theme in question and see whether it appears to be from a trusted source.

- Some authors offer free themes. They usually include a link in the footer (or elsewhere) back to the developer's website. On the face of it the deal looks sweet. NEVER use a theme that forces this type of site-wide link on you, no matter how subtle. Why? You have no control over the destination website attached to that link. The link may redirect, either now or later on, to any site the author chooses, .e.g. porn, gambling, and so on. This type of site-wide footer link will also cause you SEO problems in Google. The search engines don't like them, not even if the site it links to is a trusted one.

- Keep themes up to date and install updates as soon as you know about them. Theme developers might release an update to add new features, but it could also be to plug security holes.

# Threat 11 – Comment Spam

Comments are an important part of any WordPress website. They allow visitors to leave valuable feedback about the site's content. It's a great way to engage in a conversation with you, the webmaster, and other visitors on your website. Google likes sites that have this type of interaction. Therefore, it makes good sense to have comments enabled. There is a "but" though. Comments can also pose a real threat to your website security.

In the past, hackers have used comments to gain access to websites. They did this using something called the Zero-Day Exploit. The exploit involved hackers inserting malicious JavaScript into a simple comment. Once you approved their comment from the WordPress Dashboard, the door opened. The hacker got remote access to the site, control passwords, and add administrative users, etc. In other words, they had total control over the affected website.

If you want to research it more, this type of exploit is a good example of a "cross-scripting attack"

For the exploit to work, the webmaster had to approve the hacker's comment. That was the first hurdle for them. Fortunately for the hackers, some sites are set up to auto-approve comments IF the person had a previous comment approved.

The hacker would begin their hack by leaving a really great comment, knowing the webmaster would most likely approve it. Once accepted, they'd follow it up with a malicious comment, realizing that some sites would auto-approve it.

Look at this setting in the discussion panel:

| Before a comment appears | ☐ Comment must be manually approved |
| | ☑ Comment author must have a previously approved comment |

As things stand, if a commenter has a previously approved comment, any new ones would be auto-approved. WordPress versions between 3.9 and 4.2 were vulnerable to this hack. The developers have since patched more current versions to prevent these attacks from happening.

So now your site is up to date and safe against the Zero-Day exploit. This doesn't mean to say another, similar exploit's impossible because it's not. Hackers are smart people, and they're always looking for new ways in. For that reason, I recommend you always check the first box in that section:

**Comments must be manually approved.**

| Before a comment appears | ☑ Comment must be manually approved |
|---|---|
| | ☐ Comment author must have a previously approved comment |

Now you have to manually approve ALL comments. This way you can check the comment for code before you accept it. Moderating comments is also a good way to make sure no nasty language or hostilities end up on your pages.

## Links in Comments

When a visitor leaves a comment they have two opportunities to insert links into it. They can add a URL in the URL box of the comment section, or they can insert a link into the body of the actual comment:

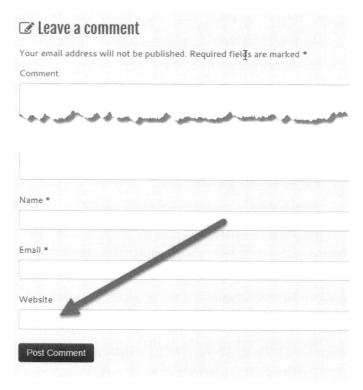

Here is a nice simple rule to follow for comments:

Always **nofollow** links in the comments section of your site. The "nofollow" attribute tells search engines not to let the link have an influence on a site's rankings. In other words, ignore it, don't follow it. You do this because you have no control over where these links point. Whoever controls the URL in the link can point it wherever they like, but you're not responsible for it.

Fortunately, the WordPress default is to nofollow links in comments. There are some plugins that give you the opportunity to make them dofollow. The advantage is that dofollow sites encourage more comments. People like them because dofollow links are valuable for off-page SEO purposes. My advice is to avoid the temptation and don't do it. If someone only leaves a comment because they want the backlink, it's likely to be a poor comment to have anyway.

Here are some other comment tips:

- Manually approve ALL comments.

- Only approve comments that genuinely add value to your page, i.e. they contribute to the conversation.

- Use a spam filter like Akismet to filter spam comments.

- Don't approve a comment if the author of the comment has filled the name field with keywords.

- Don't approve comments with links in the body of the comment unless those links point to high-authority sites you trust. If the comment is good but has unwanted links, you can always strip out the links, and then approve it.

- Never approve a comment that is trying to flatter your ego. Comments like "great post," or "cool information," are pure spam. Treat them as such.

Most comment spam tips are good common sense but it never hurts to recap.

## Threat 12 – Limit Login Attempts

When a hacker tries to get into a site, they might use special software tools. They use these to launch something called a brute force attack.

Their software programs try thousands, or hundreds of thousands, of usernames and password combinations. They can do this in a very short space of time. The way to prevent attacks of this type is to limit the number of login attempts.

If a user fails to log in after X attempts, the system locks their IP address for a set length of time. Once the time expires, they can try to log in again. It's a sensible precaution. It's there so that genuine users — who accidentally mistype their passwords — can access their site after the lockout period. As for the hackers, the delay is usually long enough for them to give up and move on to an easier target.

The plugin we install and setup in the second part of the book will limit login attempts for us. There's no need for you to do anything about it just yet.

# Threat 13 - 2-Factor Authentication

You may already have this set up for your Gmail account or another online system. It adds a great level of security to your website by requiring TWO forms of authentication.

For example, first, you go to a login form and enter your username and password (the first form of authentication). They then send a special code to your mobile phone. You then enter the code into a form (second authentication) in the login process. You can only login to your site after successfully entering the code.

It's more hassle, but it does add an extra level of security to your site, and that's always a good thing.

The plugin we install later does not offer 2-factor authentication. If you want to add this to your site, you have other options. I recommend you search the WordPress plugin repository for "Google Authenticator".

You'll find a lot of plugins that offer this functionality. Look for one with good reviews and with recent updates. Here's a good example:

This plugin is free for one user. If you want to protect more than one site, you'll need to sign up for one of their plans or find a different plugin.

After you install and activate it, you'll see a new menu item in the sidebar labeled miniOrange 2-Factor. When you click on that it takes you to a simple setup screen.

I won't go into details on how to set this up, but it's fairly intuitive. On the Setup Two-Factor tab, you can select the method of the verification, including:

- Email
- SMS
- Phone Call verification

Is this type of protection worth setting up?  Well, that's up to you. I personally find it a little too much hassle, so I don't use it on my websites.

# Threat 14 – Login Page Protection

The login page for your website is the main gateway to access your Dashboard. It's often the first port of call for hackers.

If you protect your login page, you reduce the chance of a hacker gaining access.

Fortunately, there are a few ways to protect the login page. You can rename it, move it, add a Captcha, or block certain IP addresses.

Some methods of protection are more effective than others. The plugin we install in the last part of this book gives us some great options, so no need to worry about this right now.

## Threat 15 – Database Table Prefix

Earlier in the book, we looked at backing up your WordPress websites. You saw how this was the only way to protect your site 100% from any major issues. If you remember, there were two elements to back up, namely:

1. Site files
2. Site database

WordPress uses a MySQL database that contains a number of "tables". Tables are simply spreadsheets of data. WordPress uses a number of these tables to store related information.

For example, the "users" table contains data about the users, like username and password, email address, and so on.

The "posts" table will have all the posts you've ever created. It will include date, excerpt, post name, title, and content, etc.

Each table in the database has a name, and WordPress creates these names at the install stage. You do have some control over the name of each table as these names have a prefix. WordPress, by default, used the prefix: wp_

In the case of the "users table" the name will be wp_users.

The security problem arises when the webmaster uses this default prefix. If a hacker knows your prefix, they know the name of every table in your database. Because of this, it's vital you change your default prefix.

You're in luck if you use Softaculous to install WordPress on your server. It randomly generates a prefix for your install. That means no more wp_ default.

Don't worry if you have an existing site that still uses the wp_ prefix. The plugin we install and setup later in the book gives you an easy way to change it.

# Threat 16 – WordPress Security Keys & Salts

WordPress developers introduced security keys in version 2.6, and they've been with us ever since. They initially added them to encrypt the cookie information stored on the visitor's computer.

As WordPress evolved they added more and more of these security keys. You can find them in the wp-config.php file. Automated WordPress installer software generates these for you during the install process.

You need these keys because they add an extra layer of security to your site. They encrypt vital information like passwords.

```
/**#@+
 * Authentication Unique Keys and Salts.
 *
 * Change these to different unique phrases!
 * You can generate these using the {@link https://api.wordpress.org/secret-key/1.1/salt/ WordPress
 * You can change these at any point in time to invalidate all existing cookies. This will force al
 *
 * @since 2.6.0
 */
define('AUTH_KEY',          '%DfrGM|RTU|(%+RPe^#|^F/}g#y0vq6BdN6@I-&979G4Qmq&]n)!9qop|~GHmS76');
define('SECURE_AUTH_KEY',   '(rkUuK~&3@qI;T#`ZEvF)^,/boL60`zy^#7/|Lb&lhiD-tWq%0b`H,y?^nnI*5fQ');
define('LOGGED_IN_KEY',     'cs`y7Lfy++54H1>,:ag^d1sA8&J%;Su^=]pB|5,auPR@;3a*8Z8zx8w<%JdCZz|!');
define('NONCE_KEY',         'R`)~o40U?7kx4}W5+M6#)q8iFw1uNJH`uzufMo+}o+|O*%-4~EX~~HLH+OJO:d-,');
define('AUTH_SALT',         'qn0>)&!f}1;f-Y^4__~{vaub9Bx.cDM#Z2UAxJM]C^exGzX4ecbiq%-2CI*B|h/s');
define('SECURE_AUTH_SALT',  'DNRoy1G9=)87XP-;t%{h)1-oN60|,?C@,wD)mZ;tjPd/E%pGm))nj4JS)ph:VG9c');
define('LOGGED_IN_SALT',    'oMq2`KNx16-yFs73`#bn7-5_pS=577|AN([cFBU.nSA ]#E<a=R6Fz|$yF|La?,q');
define('NONCE_SALT',        'FgY+-68>btC(9w:ID;OEXQpE~iiu@oL6$*mzY+PBaDw:;`{Gz>:e`1QU?hr|R)?i');

/**#@-*/

/**
 * WordPress Database Table prefix.
 *
```

If you install WordPress manually, you'll need to generate them yourself and copy them into the wp-config.php file. There's a URL included in the wp-config-sample.php file that generates your own unique keys & salts.

A WordPress salt is simply a random string of data. What it does is hashes (transforms) the WordPress security keys in the wp-config.php file. These security keys & salts are long. Fortunately, you don't need to remember them.

There's good news if you already have WordPress installed. These keys are more than likely already generated and residing in your wp-config.php file. If they're not, you can add them in manually, though this won't be necessary with automated installers. The only time you need to add them by hand is if you manually install WordPress. Few people have reasons to take the manual route these days.

# Threat 17 - XML-RPC

XML-RPC is a programming interface (API). What it does is allow programmers and developers to talk to WordPress.

A lot of tools may need XML-RPC to work properly. For example, I use Open Live Writer to work offline on my websites. This gives me a WYSIWYG (What You See Is What You Get) editor. I use it to create and format posts or pages that I can then publish to my site when I'm ready. Open Live Writer requires XML-RPC to be enabled for it to work.

Some plugins also need XML-RPC, like Jetpack.

Since WordPress 3.5, XML-RPC is enabled by default.

The problem we have is that software can manipulate WordPress through the XML-RPC. This makes it a possible security concern. In fact, a lot of WordPress gurus recommend you disable it.

In the past, hackers used XML-RPC for something called DDoS attacks. It stands for "Denial of Service."

Disable XML-RPC

★★★★★ (15)

This plugin disables XML-RPC API in WordPress 3.5+, which is enabled by default.

Philip Erb

80,000+ active installs          Tested with 4.7.5

Disable XML-RPC Pingback

★★★★☆ (11)

Stops abuse of your site's XML-RPC by simply removing some methods used by attackers. While you can use the rest of XML-RPC methods.

Samuel Aguilera

70,000+ active installs          Tested with 4.4.10

Plugins like Akismet can usually spot this type of attack and prevent it. Therefore, it may not be worth switching off XML-RPC to stop DDoS attacks.

Hackers also extensively used XML-RPC for brute force attacks. But again, most security plugins will prevent this type of attack today, so it's not worth worrying about. The plugin we setup later also prevents this type of attack.

My suggestion is not to disable it. If you decide you want to, then there are plugins that can disable it for you. Check out "Disable XML-RPC Pingback" and "Disable XML-RPC".

# Threat 18 - Web Hosting

The threat most people don't even think about is the hosting company they use for their website. You need to do a few checks and be aware that the cheapest option is not always the best.

If a web host offers really cheap hosting, it can mean the following:

- Plenty of people who want cheap hosting will be signing up.

- Accepts any type of site, meaning your website may be on the same server as porn, gambling, and other undesirable topics. These may be more vulnerable to hacking attempts because of their content.

- They will likely cut a few corners. Security costs money so it could be one of the weaker aspects of your host.

At the very least, you should:

- Check what version of PHP and MySQL (or MariaDB) the web host uses. These are both required for WordPress sites and should be kept up to date. This minimizes the chance of any security breaches.

- Ask your host what other security measures they take to protect your website. Do they regularly back their servers up? And in the event of a disaster, would they reinstate your site for free or a fee? How often do they carry out server maintenance? Anything specific to prevent hackers?

If you have an interest in my personal recommendation(s), you can see which host I currently use here:

http://ezseonews.com/dwh

That page will always show my up to date recommendations. I haven't changed hosts for several years now, though, as I've found a good reliable one. Therefore, don't expect the page to change any time soon.

## Threat 19 – wp-config.php

The wp-config.php file contains sensitive information. This includes things like security keys & salts, usernames, passwords, and database names, etc.

If a hacker gets hold of this file, they'd be a lot closer to hacking into your site. For this reason alone it's a good idea to protect the file in any way you can.

One way to do this is to move the file to a folder above your WordPress installation directory. Some people will tell you this is a good idea, while other security experts will disagree. I personally don't do this.

An alternative is to put the following code into the .htaccess file for your website.

<files wp-config.php>
order allow, deny
deny from all
</files>

Like this:

```
<files wp-config.php>
order allow, deny
deny from all
</files>

# BEGIN WordPress
<IfModule mod_rewrite.c>
RewriteEngine On
RewriteBase /
RewriteRule ^index\.php$ - [L]
RewriteCond %{REQUEST_FILENAME} !-f
RewriteCond %{REQUEST_FILENAME} !-d
RewriteRule . /index.php [L]
</IfModule>

# END WordPress
```

A Mac hides the .htaccess file by default, so you'll need to "unhide" all files to find it on your server.

Adding the above code will stop anyone from accessing this file. If you need to open it, you can do that via your cPanel's File Manager or FTP.

So should you add this code to your .htaccess file?

I don't, but that's my personal choice. I don't add it because the plugin we install later adds so many other good layers of protection. Because of this, I think both the above methods are unnecessary.

# Threat 20 – File Permissions

Files on a web server, just like files on a computer, have certain permissions. These permissions define who or what can access, read and/or write to those files.

Obviously, your files need tight controls. We don't want a hacker to come along and be able to access them, or worst still, change them around.

The permissions you see on a web host are a little different to what you see on a PC. Your typical PC files will have something like read-only or writable. On a web server, you'll see the permissions as numbers.

I took the following screenshot from an FTP program. Here it shows the file permissions on one of my WordPress files:

You can see that there are three groups that have permissions:

1. Owner
2. Group
3. Others

The possible permissions for each of these groups of users are:

- R – Read
- W -Write
- X – Execute (or run the file).

Note that the permission for this file is 0644 (in the 'Octal' box). So 644 is a number made up from the permissions table above. Each of these permissions has a value.

Example: For owners, the Read permission has a value of 400 and a Write value of 200. Execute would add 100 points to this permissions value.

For "Group", the Read permission has a value of 40 and a Write a value of 20. You may be able to guess the execute permission for the group has a value of 10.

For "Others", Read, Write and Execute are an order of 10 smaller, so 4, 2 and 1 respectively.

In the screenshot above, you can do the simple maths. We have:

- Owner read (400) and write (200) = 600 total.
- Groups read (40) = 40 total.
- Others read (4) = 4 total.

Therefore, the total permission for this file is 600+40+4 = 644

Fortunately, you don't need to remember any of this. I'll give you a guide to what permissions your files and folders should have, and you can check them if you want. The security plugin we install later checks and fixes permission issues for you anyway. There's nothing for you to do at the moment.

## Expected File Permissions

- All directories should be 755.
- All files should be 644, including the wp-config.php, .htaccess and wp-admin/index.php files.

OK, on that note we've now finished this section of the book. You now know the majority of security issues that relate to WordPress and how to fix them. In the second part of the book we install and setup a single security plugin. This will protect your WordPress site against most threats discussed so far.

## SECTION 2 - Secure Your Website with a Plugin

The first part of this book was an introduction to the types of protection you should use on your website. Some of these measures are a little technical to put into place. Fortunately, there's a great WordPress plugin that'll add most of these layers. Best of all is that it uses a simple point and click interface. In this section of the book, we install our smart security plugin and configure it for your site.

# Chapter 5 - Installing the Plugin

The plugin I recommend is called the "All In One WP Security & Firewall" plugin. You can find it by clicking the 'Add New' link in the Plugins menu and searching for it. This is what it looks like:

Install and activate it now.

You'll see a "WP Security" menu item in the Dashboard. If you move your mouse over WP Security, the popup menu looks like this:

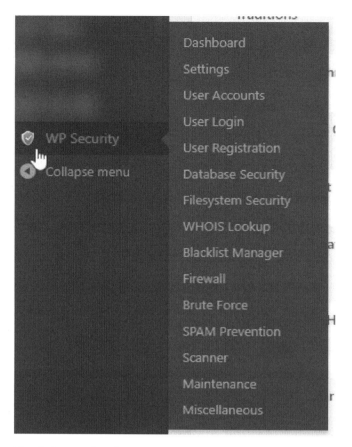

Each item in the popup menu opens a page of settings you can change.

Click on the "Dashboard" link in the menu. You'll get a graphical interpretation of the current security measures on your site.

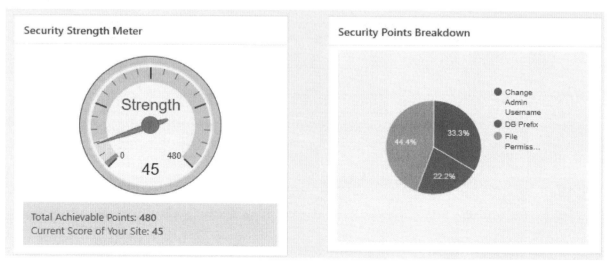

On the left, we have the "Security Strength Meter."

Currently, my sample site has a strength reading of 45 out of a possible 480. It's not great, but I've seen worse scores with this plugin installed on other sites.

On the right is a breakdown of the main security measures on my site.

Both of these graphics will look a lot different by the time we're finished.

Before we start to make any changes to the site's security, there's one very important task you need to do...

# Chapter 6 - Backup Important Files

This plugin makes changes to some of the WordPress files on your server. These changes are necessary to keep hackers out. In rare cases, though, they could break your site, or make it difficult for you to login to the Dashboard.

Don't panic, it's quite uncommon for this to happen. Even so, we're going to make backups of important files before we start. This is just a precaution in case anything goes wrong. In the event of any problems, you can simply use the backups to restore the file that causes issues.

The good news is that once you find a configuration that works for you, you won't have any problems down the line. In other words, the only time you may encounter issues is when you initially set up the plugin. We're going to go through things in some detail, and I'll inform you of any potential problems along the way. I'll also show you how to recover your site if a setting in the plugin breaks something.

You can back up all the important files from within the plugin itself. From the WP Security menu, select **Settings**.

In the WP Security Plugin section on the General Settings tab you'll see what needs backing up:

---

**WP Security Plugin**

Thank you for using our WordPress security plugin. There are a lot of security features in this plugin.

Go through each menu items and enable the security options to add more security to your site. Start by

It is a good practice to take a backup of your .htaccess file, database and wp-config.php file before acti backup those resources easily.

- o  Backup your database
- o  Backup .htaccess file
- o  Backup wp-config.php file

---

The three essential items to back up are:

- Database
- .htaccess file
- wp-config.php file

With backups of these three things, we can recover from any problem we may encounter during the plugin setup stages.

# Backup the Database

Click the link to **Back up your database**. This will open a new tab in your browser and take you to the DB Backup tab within the plugin settings.

Click the button to '**Create a DB Backup Now**.'

Once the backup is complete, you'll get a message on the screen to show you where the backed up file is on your server:

I suggest you login to your web space — via FTP or File Manager in cPanel — and download the backup to your computer. Once done, go back to the general settings tab of the plugin and click the second link to **Backup .htaccess file**.

Again, this will open a new tab in your browser. You'll see the **Backup .htaccess File** button, so click on that.

You'll get a message to confirm a successful backup and its location. Download the file to the same folder on your computer as the database backup.

Finally, click the **Backup wp-config.php file** button to open a new tab with an option to back up this file. In this case, the file downloads automatically to your computer. I suggest you then copy it to the same folder as your database and .htaccess files.

Now you have the three important files safely on your computer in case of a problem.

In the next chapter, we look at the steps to take if the plugin locks you out of your website.

# Chapter 7 - If You Get Locked Out

Locked out of your WordPress Dashboard? Don't worry! You can quickly return your website back to its previous state. We can do this by restoring one or two files. I'll show you how to do that now.

You can work with the files on your server in a couple of ways:

- FTP (File Transfer Protocol, using an FTP Client software tool).
- File Manager in cPanel.

Personally, I like to use FTP. It's faster and more convenient than going through the cumbersome File Manager inside cPanel. If you don't know how to set FTP up for your web server, ask your web host. Alternatively, you can always use the File Manager inside cPanel to make the necessary changes.

## IP Lockout

One of the main reasons the plugin locks people out is if their IP address triggers the security settings. If it locks your IP address, you won't be able to login to your Dashboard with that particular IP.

The simplest solution is to use a tool like Zenmate VPN:

http://ezseonews.com/zenmate

This lets you change the IP on your computer as if you were in a different location, even a different country.

When the system logged me out in the past, the first thing I would do is change my IP using Zenmate VPN (Virtual Private Network). I'd then log in and make the necessary changes to the plugin settings. I'd say this works fine in 99% of all cases, without the need to restore any files.

If you don't want to buy Zenmate or similar, then you'll need to restore backup files to regain access to your Dashboard.

## Restoring Files

The problem with restoring files is that you lose all customizations to the plugin settings since the last backup. In other words, say you took the backup before you began to configure the plugin. This means — after the restoration — you'll have to reconfigure it all again from the start.

One thing that can make life a little easier is if you back up the files periodically as you set up the plugin. Then, if a problem does arise, you can restore the files starting with the most recent backup. If necessary, you can work backward until you find the backup file that fixes the issue.

So you need your backup files to restore your site in the event of a problem. We saved those to your computer in the last chapter.

The chance is you'll only need to restore the .htaccess file as it's where the plugin makes most of its changes. If WordPress does lock you out, I recommend you try to restore functionality in the following order:

1. Restore .htaccess file and check to see if you can get in. If you can, you don't need to follow step 2. If you can't, keep reading.

2. Restore wp-config.php file and check to see if you can get in.

After completing steps one and two, you should have access to your site. If not, then clear cookies in your browser and try again.

If you still can't get in, I recommend you go and rename your "plugins" folder. This is the last resort, but it does work. You can then log in, but you'll get some error messages. Ignore them. While you're logged in, rename the plugins folder back to its correct name and refresh the browser. You should now be able to access the Security settings and make the changes.

I've never seen an instance where you'd need to restore the database because of the security plugin. The database backup is very useful in case your site gets hacked and you need to restore the content. However, for a full backup I recommend you look at a plugin like Updraft:

http://ezseonews.com/updraft

## Restoring the .htaccess file

This is simply a matter of uploading your backup and overwriting the existing .htaccess file in the root folder of your site.

First, it's worth having a look at the .htaccess file on your server. You'll see it contains some comments that pinpoint the changes made by the plugin:

```
# BEGIN All In One WP Security
#AIOWPS_BASIC_HTACCESS_RULES_START
<Files .htaccess>
<IfModule mod_authz_core.c>
Require all denied
</IfModule>
<IfModule !mod_authz_core.c>
Order deny,allow
Deny from all
```

Comments start with the # symbol.

As you can see, the block of code added to the htaccess file begins with:

# BEGIN All In One WP Security

...and ends with:

# END All In One WP Security

```
Require not env bad_bot
</RequireAll>
</IfModule>
</IfModule>
#AIOWPS_SIX_G_BLACKLIST_END
# END All In One WP Security
```

Another way to try and recover your site is by reinstating your .htaccess file by deleting all the plugin content. This is the code that starts with the opening **# BEGIN All In One WP Security** and ends with **# END All in One WP Security**. Make sure you save the edited file back to your server.

This should remove all security measures applied by the plugin.

If you don't want to manually edit this file, then simply restore the backup.

To do this:

1. Upload your backup to the root folder of your web site.
2. Delete the original.
3. Rename your backup (which will have a random name created during its backup) to .htaccess.

If you are not sure which is the root folder of your site, you can quickly identify it because it contains the following WordPress folders (yellow highlight):

You can also see the original .htaccess file in the root folder. For Mac users, the .htaccess file is probably invisible by default, so you'll need to unhide it to see it.

After you restore the backup .htaccess file, you should have access to your site again through the regular login URL.

If you don't, you can use the same procedure to restore the wp-config.php file.

You should then get access back to your Dashboard. Now you can start to set up the plugin again.

# Chapter 8 – Classification of Security Measures

To make things easier and safer, the plugin classifies its security measures into three categories:

1. Basic
2. Intermediate
3. Advanced

The **Basic** classification means it will not break your site.

The **Intermediate** classification means it can cause problems, but usually it's fine.

The **Advanced** classification means be careful! This could break your site.

## Our Security Strategy Going Forward

The best strategy is to activate all the basic measures immediately. These should be totally safe and will give your site a lot of protection against hackers.

After activating these, make a new backup of your files (the same ones as earlier). I suggest you save them to a separate folder (maybe call it "postbasic").

If you have to restore the files, you can use these "postbasic" ones. It's a simple system that means you won't have to configure the plugin again from scratch.

My advice is to test the site for a day or two to make sure everything works fine.

You can then go in and activate some of the intermediate measures, and again take a backup of the files once you're done. Put these into a separate folder (maybe call this one "postinter").

Again, you'll test the site for a couple of days to make sure there are no issues.

You can then go in and activate some of the "Advanced" features.

At any stage, if you have problems, you can go back and restore the files. Just choose the ones from the last working configuration before you implemented the advanced strategies.

In the next few chapters, we'll go through all the setup screens and most of the options: Basic, Intermediate and Advanced. I'll tell you the settings I recommend you enable. Some of these will be Basic, some Intermediate and a few Advanced.

The first time you go through these chapters, only activate the basic features I suggest. Once activated and working fine, backup the files and work through the chapters again. This time, enable my recommended "Intermediate" features. After a day or two, back up the files and work your way through these chapters again.

This time you'll enable my recommended "Advanced" features. This is our strategy.

There are a couple of settings that I know cause issues for some people. These can trigger the IP lockouts we looked at earlier. I'll highlight those for you as we go through the settings. If the system locks you out, once you get access again, go and disable the known troublemakers first. Then log out of your site and back in again. You can then start to re-enable these settings one at a time and test them for a day or two before moving on.

OK, let's begin by looking at the Dashboard screen.

# Chapter 9 – The Dashboard

If you click on **Dashboard** in the **WP Security** menu, the Dashboard screen loads. Across the top, as with many of these settings pages, you'll see a few tabs:

Here we have the Dashboard tab selected. From this tab, you can see two graphical representations of your current security strength.

The first one is a dial, from zero to 480.

480 is the maximum achievable score, though you won't actually get that high. At the 6 O'clock position you can see my current score of 45.

The other graphic on this page is a pie chart. This includes a few segments which represent the security measures currently in force.

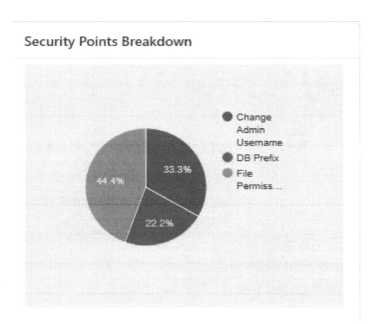

Security Points Breakdown

This pie chart gets more cluttered as you add extra security measures to your site.

Before you start, I recommend you record your security strength meter score. You can then compare it to your optimal score at the end of this book.

Have a look down at the other information on this Dashboard screen. An interesting item is the **Critical Feature Status**. This shows the enabled status for a few of the more critical features:

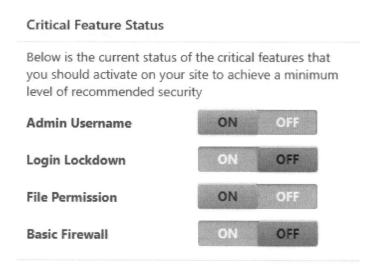

Critical Feature Status

In my case, there's no login lockdown or basic firewall used. These are two highly recommended security features.

You have two ways to activate these. The first is to use the sub-menus on the **WP-Security** sidebar to access the correct settings page. For example, you'll find the basic firewall on the **Firewall** settings page.

A quicker way, though, is to simply click the "switch" on the **Critical Feature Status** panel. Do that now.

By clicking the **Login Lockdown** switch, the system automatically takes you to the settings page that contains the login lockdown feature.

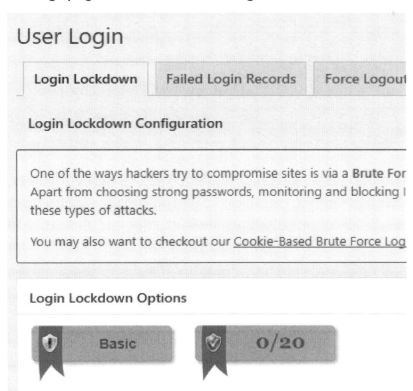

As you can see, this is on the **User Login** settings page, which you can also access from the main **WP-Security** menu.

This screen also has tabs, and you can see a section for **Login Lockdown Options**. Currently, we score 0 out of a possible 20 points.

OK, let's set up the login lockdown.

There's a badge that tells you this is a 'Basic' security measure. It means there's almost zero chance of it causing any issues. To activate the login lockdown, simply check the **Enable Login Lockdown Feature** box.

There are a few other options you can set up with this. I recommend you leave all the other settings at their default values. There are helpful hints next to each check box if you want to know what each one does.

The only item on that list you might want to think about is the **Max Login Attempts**. Ask yourself whether you frequently mistype the wrong username or password. If no, then you may want to reduce this from 3 to 2. Or set it to 1 if you use a password tool for entering passwords as there won't be any accidental login attempts. This setting tells the plugin when to lock a user out of your login page. If it's set to 1, when a visitor or hacker tries once and fails, the system automatically blocks their IP.

You can also specify how long you want to lock someone out for before they can try again. Here, 60 minutes is the default and is probably a good time to use. This is plenty long enough to deter hackers. But it's short enough so that you don't lose a whole day of work if the system accidentally locks you out.

You can setup auto email notifications to inform you of any failed login attempts. Just enter an email address at the end of the form and you're set.

At the bottom of the settings page you can see a **Whitelist**. This is useful if you want to make sure a certain IP address always gets to login without issues. You can enter an IP address or range of IPs into the box. My advice is to only do this if you know what your IP will be every time you turn on your computer.

When you're happy with the settings, click the **Save Settings** button.

The **User Login** screen will reload and you'll see you've scored 20 out of 20 for the login lockdown feature. Click on the **Dashboard** link to go back to the Dashboard.

Now recheck your security strength:

You can see how mine has increased by 20 points to 65. You can also see a new pie on the right-hand diagram. I now have four security measures in place.

The other "critical issue" from the **Critical Feature Status** we need to resolve is the **Basic Firewall**:

We have a green light now for login lockdown switch.

Now click on the **Basic Firewall** switch, to open the firewall settings:

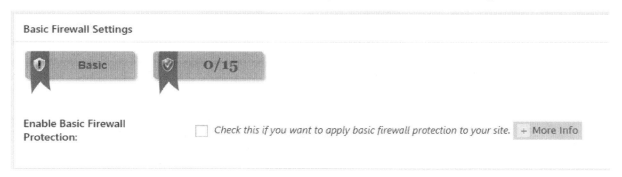

This screen has a few tabs across the top, and we'll come back to look at these later. For now, you can see my score for **Basic Firewall Settings** is 0 out of 15.

You can also see the "Basic" badge, so this setting is safe to use.

Check the box to enable the basic firewall. Now scroll to the bottom and click the **Save Basic Firewall Settings** button.

Return to the Dashboard again to check your new security score:

Security Strength Meter

Strength

80

0    480

Total Achievable Points: 480
Current Score of Your Site: 80

Security Points Breakdown

- Change Admin Username
- Login Lockdown
- DB Prefix
- File Permiss...
- Enable Basic Firewall

18.8%  18.8%
25%    25%

As you can see, every new security measure you enable, the security on the site gets stronger.

There is one more thing I want to show you on the Dashboard tab. Look for the **Maintenance Mode Status** panel.

The current status is set to OFF, and you want to keep it off. Switching it on enables WordPress maintenance mode and your site becomes unavailable to visitors. They'll get a message—something you can define yourself. There may be times when you want to enable this, e.g. when you're doing work you don't want others to see. It's not something I've ever used, but you may find it useful.

OK, that's the Dashboard tab covered. You'll also see a few other tabs across the top. I won't go into details on these as we don't need them to setup your security. You can click on each one just to see what's there.

### 1. System Info

This provides some information about your website, server, and any software running on the server. For example, you may want to know what version of PHP your host is running. This screen gives you the information you need.

### 2. Locked IP Addresses

As the name suggests, this lists any current and temporarily locked out IP addresses. These would include any IP addresses locked out because of invalid login attempts.

### 3. Permanent Block list

This shows a list of all the permanently blocked IPs from your site.

### 4. AIOWPS Logs

AIOWPS stands for 'All In One WordPress Security.' This screen gives you access to any log files used by the plugin. You can examine them if you need to troubleshoot, for example. Most users won't ever need to look at these.

This concludes our **Dashboard** settings.

# Chapter 10 - Settings

Click on **Settings** in the **WP-Security** menu.

Earlier in the book we created backups of important files. We created these backups using with the **Settings** options. If you look at the tabs across the top of the **Settings** screen, you probably recognize them.

The **General Settings** tab provides links to back up the following:

1. Database
2. .htaccess file
3. Wp-config.php file

A useful feature on this screen is one we've not looked at yet. It's the **Disable Security Features** button.

**Disable Security Features**

> If you think that some plugin functionality on your site is broken due to a security feature you enabled in this plugin, then use the following option to turn off all the security features of this plugin.

Disable All Security Features

This button turns off all security measures enabled in the plugin. It's useful if you have problems with your site and can still log into the Dashboard. The killer switch resets all security measure back to their default settings. In my case, my security score would return to 45.

Another option you have here is to **Disable All Firewall Rules**. It's a less extreme measure to use if you think the issue relates to your firewall settings. It will delete all firewall settings from your site's .htaccess file and thus disable the firewall.

Finally, at the bottom of the screen is the **Debug Settings**. It turns on the debug mode and creates a log file, which can then help you to debug difficult situations.

The second tab on the **Settings** screen is the .htaccess file tab. This screen lets you back up your .htaccess file and restore one if you need to. If you can't login to the Dashboard to restore the file, you can log in via FTP or File Manager in cPanel. It's then just a case of uploading the one you want to restore.

The wp-config.php tab allows you to backup and restore this file if necessary.

Now click on the **WP Version Info** tab.

One of the things hackers like to know is the version of WordPress you use for your site. If they know you're using version 4.6, for example, they can check what vulnerabilities exist with that particular version. They can then get to work and exploit those vulnerabilities. For some reason, WordPress likes to give this information out to anyone who wants it. They do this by including the info in the source code for every page on your site.

This plugin lets you remove that info by disabling the **WP Generator Meta Info**:

WP Generator Meta Info

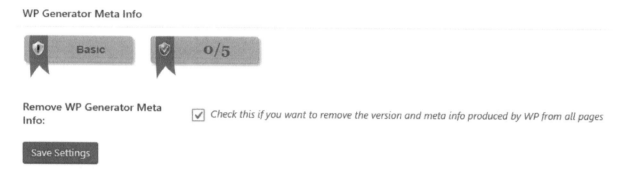

Remove WP Generator Meta Info:

☑ *Check this if you want to remove the version and meta info produced by WP from all pages*

Save Settings

It's a "Basic" feature, so it's safe to implement. Check the box and click **Save Settings**. Your security score will go up by another 5 points.

The final tab in **Settings** is the **Import/Export** tab.

This screen allows you to export all your AIOWPS settings.

### Export AIOWPS Settings

*To export your All In One WP Security & Firewall settings click the button below.*

Export AIOWPS Settings

Once you've exported the settings, you can then import them into your new site from this tab.

**Import AIOWPS Settings**

*Use this section to import your All In One WP Security & Firewall settings from a file. Alternatively, copy/paste the contents of your import file into the textarea below.*

Import File:

> Select Your Import Settings File
>
> *After selecting your file, click the button below to apply the settings to your site.*

Copy/Paste Import Data:

Import AIOWPS Settings

## Settings #1 – User Accounts

Click on the **User Accounts** link in the **WP Security** menu. You'll see three tabs.

The first tab is **WP Username**. This is a simple check to make sure you're not using "admin" as your username. If you are, you shouldn't be.

In my case, I'm not using "admin" but I've created a second user who does, just so I can show you what to expect. You can skip this setting if you already have 15 points for a non-admin username.

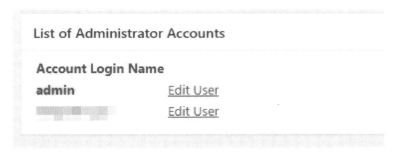

You can see two users in my demo (one blurred out).

I've logged in as the admin user, and further down the page I see this message:

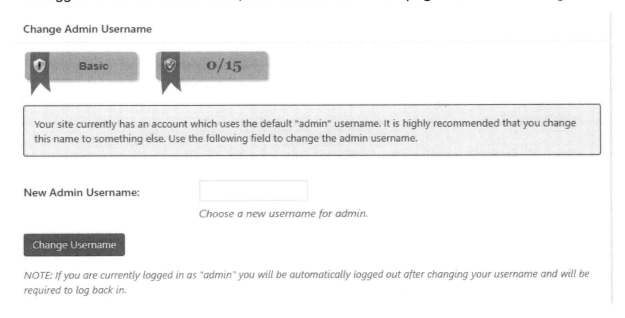

I get 0 out of 15 because my username is **admin**.

It's easy to change. I simply need to enter a new username in the box provided and then click **Change Username**.

The Dashboard then logs you out once you've changed your username.

Now you can log back in with your new username and old password.

You now get the 15 points allocated for a non-admin username.

The second tab on the **User Accounts** settings is **Display Name**. When you publish content on your site, WordPress displays your "nickname." Your nickname is your login name by default. This is a bad idea for security reasons.

This setting in the plugin allows you to change your nickname (display name).

If your display name and username are the same, you get a warning:

You can also see it's a "Basic" security measure, so it's safe to implement. At the moment I've got a 0 score for this.

To change a display name, click the link of the username. The system then takes you to the profile page of the user. This is where you can select a different name in the **Display name publicly as** section:

The **display name** options you have come from the fields: username, first name, last name, and nickname.

Select a name and then click **Update Profile**.

When you go back to the **User Accounts** settings, **Display Name** tab, you'll see 5/5:

Modify Accounts With Identical Login Name & Display Name

The final tab in the **User Account** settings is **Password**.

The password setting is not for changing your password but to check its strength. Use this tool to see if your password needs to be stronger (see image):

That's the **User Accounts** settings complete.

Back in the Dashboard, my security score has now gone up to 90, and the pie chart is starting to look a little more impressive.

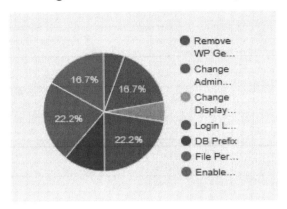

There's still a long way to go, though.

## Settings #2 – User Login

The next settings page is the **User Login** screen. This comes with a few useful tabs across the top:

The first tab is one we visited earlier– **Login Lockdown**. We've already configured those settings. There's another option I want to highlight, and that's the ability to lock out usernames.

It's interesting when you start to get information about who's trying to hack into your website. You can see how hackers attempt all manner of usernames to gain access. A lot of them will obviously try "admin," but they'll try a lot of other educated guesses too. The best defense here is to lock out invalid usernames.

This plugin gives us that opportunity.

**Instantly Lockout Invalid Usernames:**

☐ *Check this if you want to instantly lockout login attempts with usernames which do not exist on your system*

**Instantly Lockout Specific Usernames:**

*Insert one username per line. Existing usernames are not blocked even if present in the list.*

Check the box to **Instantly Lockout Invalid Usernames**. Then, if someone tries to login with a username that doesn't correspond to a real user, they're blocked.

The box under this checkbox allows you to block specific usernames. With a tick in the above checkbox, though, you don't need to worry about individual usernames.

The next tab is the **Failed Login Records** screen. This one shows you a list of all failed logins on your site (mostly hacking attempts). Here are the failed login records for one of my other WordPress websites:

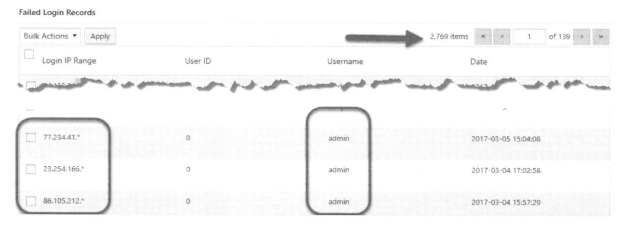

The screenshot here shows 2,796 failed login attempts. There'd be a lot more if the plugin had not locked out many of these first failed attempts.

With each record, you can see the IP address of the user who tried to access my site. If the same IP crops up a lot, you can permanently block it if you want to.

You can also see the username exploited by the would-be hacker. In those three instances, they tried to use admin. See how important it's to change it?"

The next tab is **Force Logout**. It's a "Basic" security measure so we can enable it right away:

**Force Logout** logs out an admin user after they've been in the Dashboard for X minutes (60 minutes is the default). This can be useful because if a hacker gets in by chance, the system logs them out after the set period. If you don't usually spend long in your Dashboard, you can reduce the 60-minute limit still further. It's handy because it reduces the time a hacker has to wreak havoc on your site.

Remember, the system logs you out after this time too. If it becomes a nuisance, you may want to leave the feature disabled.

If you do enable it, make sure you click the **Save Settings** button.

The **Account Activity Logs** screen displays the activity of registered accounts in your Dashboard. It shows you the last 50 logins, with username, IP, and timestamp. You should be able to recognize all of these users.

The final tab is the **Logged in Users**. It simply shows you the users logged into your Dashboard right now. You can see the login name and IP address. It's for information only.

# Setting #3 - User Registration

The **User Registration** settings are only important if you allow visitors to register on the site. If you don't know why you'd want visitors to register on your site, you most likely don't need them.

**NOTE:** If you don't want to allow visitors to register, leave the **User Registration** settings at their default values.

If you want visitors to register, make sure you manually approve all new users. This is for basic security measures.

We can enable that with this plugin.

Go to the **User Registration** settings:

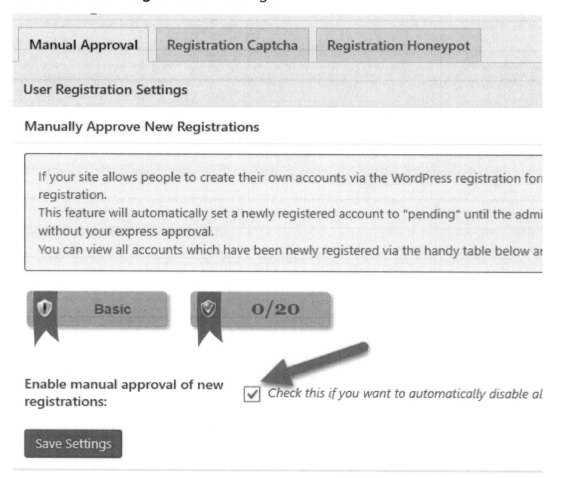

On the **Manual Approval** tab, check the **Enable manual approval of new registrations** check box (basic security classification). Now click **Save Settings**.

You can also enable a Captcha on the user registration form. This helps to cut down on automated bot registrations. To activate the Captcha, click onto the **Registration Captcha** tab. Check the box to **Enable Captcha on Registration Page**:

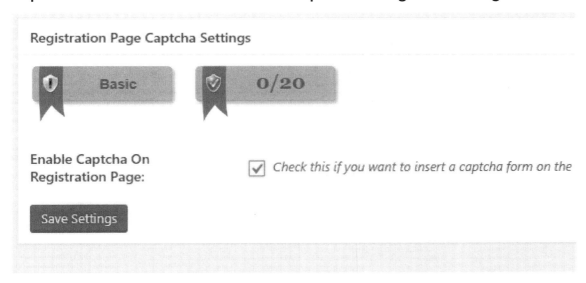

Click the **Save Settings** button.

This is another of the "Basic" security measures.

Finally, there's an "Intermediate" security measure. Click the **Registration Honeypot** tab.

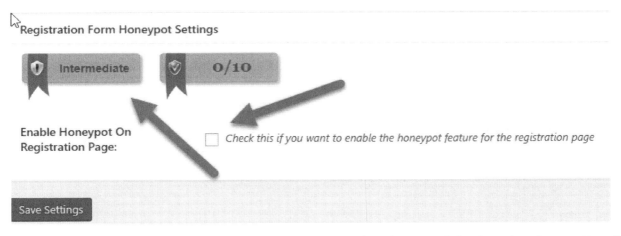

Since this is an "Intermediate" feature, you need to be careful when implementing it. As I mentioned earlier in the book, I recommend you only activate basic features the first time around. Once you're certain they're working properly, go back and activate the "Intermediate" features.

When you're done, make sure you **Save Settings**.

# Setting #4 – Database Security

The **Database Security** screen has two tabs: the **DB Prefix** and **DB Backup** screens.

On the DB Prefix screen, you can make sure your database doesn't use the old default wp_ as a prefix on your databases. If you've installed WordPress in the last year or so you should be fine. An automated installer like Softaculous will create a random prefix at the install stage.

This is an "Intermediate" feature. That means it could possibly cause some issues. If you use the plugin to change the prefix (and only do it if your prefix is wp_), there's a slim chance it might corrupt your database. I've never had a problem with this, and I suspect you won't either, but it's potentially problematic.

To be safe, there's a link for the **DB Backup** feature. I recommend you backup now, even if you only intend to activate basic features at this point. It's a good habit to get into, and backing up healthy files never hurt any site.

Once done, check the box to **Generate New DB Table Prefix** and click the **Change DB Prefix** button.

You should see a confirmation message to inform you everything went smoothly:

The other tab on the **Database Security** settings has the tools for backing up the database. At the top, you can see an option to manually back up the database:

Below is something that's really useful—an automated backup tool. This is a "Basic" security measure and adds 20 points to your score.

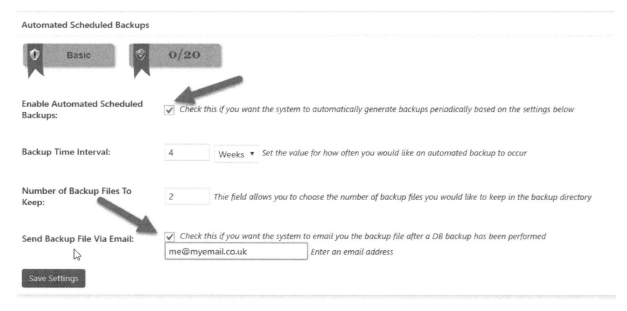

Check the box to **Enable Automated Scheduled Backups.**

You can choose how often to create backups. If you work a lot on your site, you might want weekly backups. The default is every four weeks, and that's fine for a site that doesn't add much new content each month.

You can specify how many backups to keep. The default is two, but I'd push that up to three.

Finally, if you want the backups emailed to you, check the box at the bottom and enter the email address you want to use.

Click **Save Settings** when you're done.

Now go back and check your security strength. Mine is now up to 115.

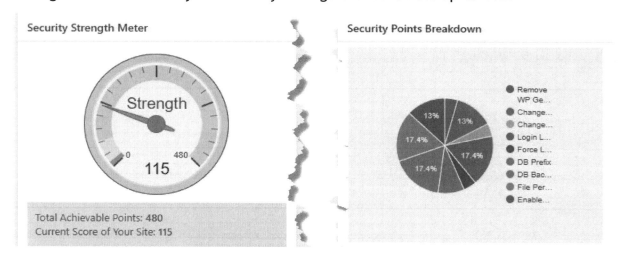

# Setting #5 – Filesystem Security

The **Filesystem Security** settings check to make sure the files and folders use the correct permissions. Remember, it's important to restrict access to your files and folders to only those systems and people who need access.

There are four tabs on the **Filesystem Security** screen.

File Permissions is the first tab. Here you'll see a table of files and folders, together with their current and recommended permissions.

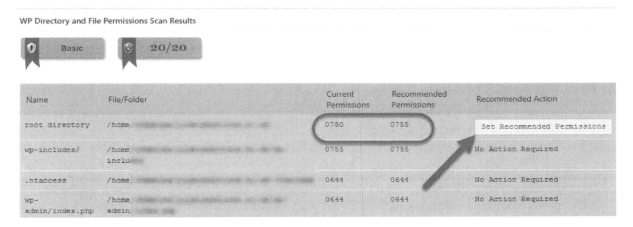

In the table above you can see the root directory of the site has permissions of 0750, but the plugin recommends 0755. You can check what this means by referring to the section earlier in the book where we discussed these numbers.

This permission setting is not a big security threat (you can see we already have 20 out of 20), but we'll fix it anyway. We can do this by clicking the **Set Recommended Permissions** button next to that entry in the table.

AIOWPS has corrected the permissions for me with a single click.

Once you've corrected permissions on your site, click the **PHP File Editing** tab.

When a hacker breaks into your Dashboard, one of the first places they go is the PHP file editor. With this tool, they can hack into the plugin and theme files. They can then change them or inject malicious code into the files.

A simple way to prevent this is to disable the PHP editor. If you — as webmaster — want to edit the PHP files at any time, you still can. All you do is access the files via FTP or File Manager in cPanel, so it's no big deal.

This is a "Basic" security measure, so is safe to do now.

Simply check the box to **Disable Ability to Edit PHP Files** and click **Save Settings.**

Now click on the **WP File Access** tab. This tab allows you to hide other files that a hacker might use to gain information about your site.

Again, it's a "Basic" security measure and therefore safe to implement right away.

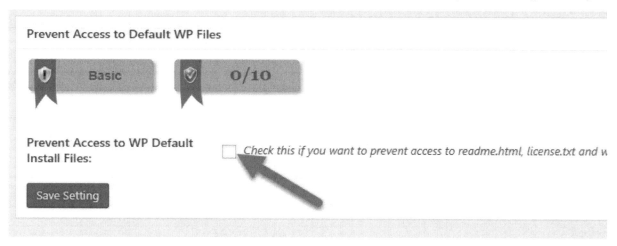

Check the box to **Prevent Access to WP Default Install Files.** Click **Save Settings.**

The final tab in these settings is the **Host System Logs.** This tab allows you to view your hosting error log files. You'll need to know the name of the files produced by your hosting server to make use of this feature.

# Setting #6 – WHOIS Lookup

The **WHOIS Lookup** feature allows you to find out a little more information about the IP addresses that try to break into your website.

If you know the IP address that attempts to break in, you can enter it into the box provided, and then click the **Perform IP or Domain Lookup** button.

You'll get a lot of information back using the Lookup feature. Here's some of the data returned for the IP above:

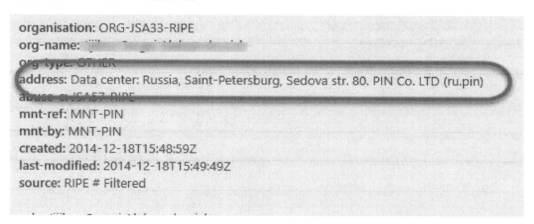

Run the IP through your own WHOIS if you want to see the full details.

# Setting #7 – Blacklist Manager

This is a really useful tool because it allows you to block IP addresses from accessing your site.

Click on the **Blacklist Manager** in the sidebar menu.

At the top of the page, you'll see something like this:

> You may also be interested in our Country Blocking Addon.
> This addon allows you to automatically block IP addresses based on their country of origin.

The plugin can block specific IP addresses, but that's not all. The **Country Blocking Addon** allows you to block entire countries if you need to. That plugin is a paid upgrade, though, and I don't cover it in this book.

You'll also notice that this security feature is an "Advanced" one. You need to use it with some caution. I recommend you activate this at a later date, once you're sure everything else is working fine. If you misuse this feature, you could find yourself locked out of your site.

To activate the blacklist, check the **Enable IP or User Agent Blacklisting** box.

You can now enter the IP address(es) you want to block. You can use a wildcard to specify a range, e.g. 31.184.238.* This blocks out all IP addresses that start with 31.184.238.

You can also enter full IP addresses:

Enter IP Addresses:

```
31.184.238.*
52.166.125.125
```

When you enter a new IP address, make sure you put each one on a separate line.

You can also block user agents. This includes all kinds of bots that roam the internet, e.g. baiduspider, SurveyBot, and so on.

**Enter User Agents:**          baiduspider
                                SquigglebotBot

You block these by entering their names in the second box.

# Setting #8 – Firewall

We activated the basic firewall when we first installed the plugin. There're a lot more firewall settings you can activate. Some are Basic measures, some are Intermediate or Advanced. Let's go through each of these.

Click on the **Firewall** menu in the left sidebar.

You'll see the firewall screen has a few tabs across the top. For now, you should be on the **Basic Firewall Rules** tab.

At the top, you can see the basic firewall enabled (we did that earlier).

Below this is another "Basic" feature:

**Point to note:** *Before you activate this feature you need to read a little further.*

The first option is to **Completely Block Access to XMLRPC.** The thing is you may need XMLRPC functionality, so to disable it could cause you problems. On the other side of the coin, XMLRPC is a common gateway for hackers. If you're not using it, I suggest you disable it.

Example: I personally use Open Live Writer (previously Windows Live Writer) to manage my blog content. It's a tool I use for writing content offline. When I'm ready, I then publish the post direct from within Open Live Writer. This tool requires XMLRPC to function. To disable it would stop Open Live Writer from working. In short, I wouldn't be able to publish content to the site because the program would no longer connect.

Another example is the Jetpack plugin. This requires XMLRPC as well. Fortunately, the plugin gives you an easy way around this problem. You can actually tell it you use Jetpack, or any other apps that need XMLRPC to work.

You have two options.

If you want to completely block XMLRPC, check the **Completely Block Access to XMLRPC** box. This overwrites the **Disable Pingback Functionality From XMLRPC** feature, so it doesn't matter what you do with that checkbox, it'll be ignored.

The second option is to allow software and plugins that need XMLRPC, but to block anything else. To achieve this, check the **Disable Pingback Functionality From XMLRPC.** Make sure the **Completely Block Access to XMLRPC** box is UNCHECKED:

The final feature on the basic firewall rules tab is **Block Access to Debug Log File.**

This is an "Intermediate" feature that prevents access to a debug log file. This file can contain sensitive information, so I recommend you eventually enable it.

When you're done with the basic rules, click on the **Additional Firewall Rules** tab.

These features are all "Intermediate" or "Advanced". I suggest you come back and activate these once you're sure your basic settings are behaving well.

The first option is to **Disable Index Views.** Some web servers allow the listing of files and folders in the web space. This isn't a great idea as it gives hackers more information about your site. My advice is to **Disable Index Views:**

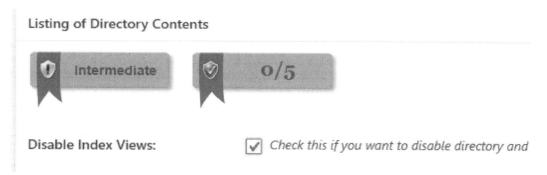

The next option lets you disable trace and track. This will prevent what's called an HTTP Trace attack.

I recommend you enable it—eventually—but it's an "Advanced" security measure, so leave it for the time being.

Next up is another "Advanced" option, but it's an important one that helps to cut down on spam. The **Proxy Comment Posting** option allows you to block comments coming in from a proxy server (used by people trying to hide their true IP address). I recommend you enable this option—eventually.

The next option is **Bad Query Strings**. You need to be careful with this one, though. Activating it may cause conflicts with certain plugins or themes. Make sure you backup your .htaccess file before you implement it. This way you can quickly revert back if there's an issue.

The final option on this screen is the **Advanced Character String Filter**. This feature can help prevent Cross Site Scripting attacks (XSS). Once again, it's an "Advanced" feature, and can break your site. Take a backup of your .htaccess file before you implement it.

When you're done, click on the **Save Additional Firewall Settings** button.

You can now go over to the **6G Blacklist Firewall Rules** tab.

When you decide to activate "Advanced" measures, I recommend you activate the 6G firewall protection on this screen:

Don't bother with the 5G. That's an older form of protection that the 6G firewall has since replaced.

The next tab in the **Firewall** settings is the **Internet Bots** tab.

This is an "Advanced" feature that aims to block malicious bots masquerading as Googlebot:

I recommend you eventually activate it. The plugin will then perform verification tests on any bot claiming to come from Google and block those that fail the tests.

OK, now save your settings and move onto the **Prevent Hotlinks** tab.

If you have images on your site, each one will have its own URL. Anyone can grab the URLs of your images and embed them onto their own sites. It's a problem not least because YOUR server serves the image wherever they are. So every time the rogue site loads one of your stolen images, it uses YOUR bandwidth.

For this reason, I recommend you activate this "Basic" feature:

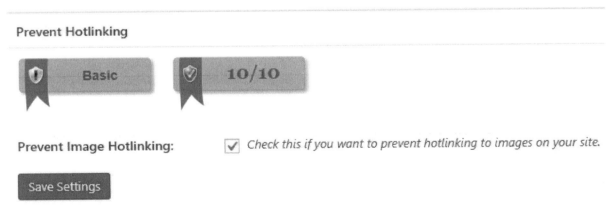

Save the settings, then click on the **404 Detection** tab.

When a visitor tries to view a page on your site that no longer exists, they'll likely see a 404 error. The message explains that the page they're looking for is no longer available. It's correct, and the way websites should function. Real visitors can innocently get to 404 pages via broken links. For example, a link that points to a page the webmaster has since moved or deleted.

The difference with hackers is that they try lots of web pages in a short space of time as they search for a download page. They'll likely come across a series of 404 errors in a matter of minutes or seconds even. This identifies them as hackers, and it's what this feature aims to do. Identify hackers and then block them.

This is an "Intermediate" feature, but I recommend you enable it—eventually.

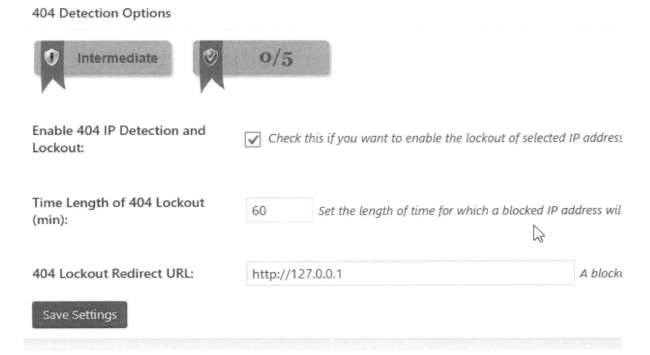

Only check the **Enable 404 IP Detection and Lockout** box and leave the other settings as they are. When the plugin identifies a hacker, it sends them to 404 Lockout Redirect URL. You can enter anything you want in that box, or just leave it at the default. It's completely up to you.

If the system locks someone out with this security measure, you'll see the details of these events in the logs on this screen.

Here are the logs for one of my sites:

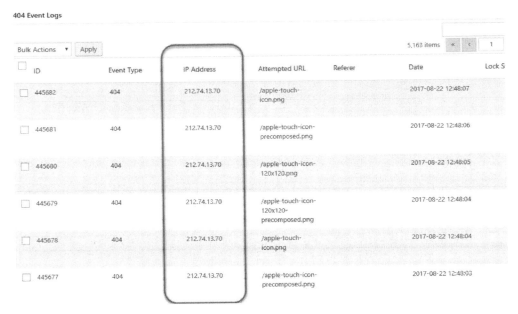

There were six 404 events by the same IP address within the space of 4 seconds! This would be a good IP address to add to my blacklist!

To block an IP, you can mouse-over the event ID to bring up a menu:

Here you get the option for a temporary block, or to blacklist the IP address.

The final tab on the **Firewall** screen is for **Custom Rules**.

This is for anyone who wants to add custom rules to the .htaccess file. These advanced techniques are beyond the scope of this book and can easily break a site.

# Setting #9 - Brute Force Protection

The **Brute Force** settings will help prevent "brute force attacks" on your website.

In my experience, these settings cause website owners the biggest problems. They'll often lock the webmaster out of their Dashboard. If you get them to work well, though, they provide a serious and powerful layer of protection.

There are a couple of really useful options. The first one is to rename the WordPress login page so that scripts and bots can't find it.

The **Rename Login Page Settings** panel is where you can rename this page. It's an "Intermediate" feature, so take care.

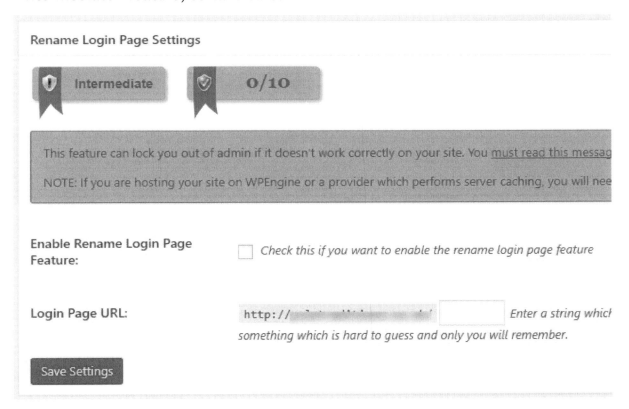

Read the warning box at the top, and click the link to read the message. If your web host uses server caching, this feature could easily break your site.

To activate it, check the **Enable Rename Login Page Feature**. Next, enter a string of characters that are hard to guess in the **Login Page URL** box.

**Save Settings** once done. You must remember your new login page URL.

Personally, I don't activate this feature. Instead, I use the **Cookie Based Brute Force Prevention** method—your second option to prevent brute force attacks.

Click on the tab of the **Brute Force** settings.

This **Cookie Based Brute Force Prevention** method is an "Advanced" feature. If you run into problems, I suggest you deactivate it and use the login page renaming method instead.

Before you activate the cookie based method, scroll to the bottom of the screen and click on the **Perform Cookie Test** button. It will check to make sure your system is capable of using this method of protection.

Hopefully, you should receive the following confirmation:

The cookie test was successful. You can now enable this feature.

Save Feature Settings

To enable this method, check the **Enable Brute Force Attacks Prevention** box. Now enter a secret word into the **Secret Word** box. It should be something that's difficult to guess and will become part of your new login URL.

Does your website have any posts or pages that are password protected? If it does, make sure you check the **My Site Has Posts or Pages which are Password Protected** box.

If your WordPress theme or plugins use Ajax, check the **My Site Has a Theme or Plugins Which Use Ajax** box.

Now click on the **Save Feature Settings** box.

At the top of the screen, you'll see confirmation that your new login page is ready, and you'll see the URL. It should look something like the one below:

http://mysite.com/?mysecretword=1

You MUST copy and save that URL to a safe place. If you lose it, you won't be able to log into your Dashboard.

The way the protection works is to write a cookie to your computer when you visit that URL. That URL then redirects you to your login page. But if the cookie's not on your computer, you won't be able to log in, not even with the correct username and password.

Imagine a hacker comes to your login page. Even if they know your username and password, they still can't access your site if they haven't visited your secret URL first to pick up the cookie. That's pretty cool.

The next tab on the **Brute Force** settings is the **Login Captcha** screen.

You'll find three "Basic" features on this screen that you can activate if you want.

These put a captcha on the login form, custom login form, and lost password form respectively.

Captchas can help reduce brute force attacks because logins require a mathematical problem to be solved.

Check all three boxes and save the settings.

The next tab is the **Login Whitelist** screen.

This screen lets you specify which IP addresses (or range of addresses) you allow to log into your Dashboard. If you use this feature, it'll block all other, unspecified, IP addresses. It's an "Intermediate" feature, so use it with caution. It works by writing directly to your .htaccess file, so back that up before you enable it.

Personally, I don't use this feature and nor do I recommend you use it either, unless you know what you're doing.

The last tab in the **Brute Force** settings is the **Honeypot**. This is a clever protection method that shows a hidden "honeypot" field on the login page to all bots. Human visitors don't see it, but bots do. They then fill in the "honeypot" field, and the plugin knows it's a bot.

This is an "Intermediate" measure, but I do recommend you enable it—eventually.

# Setting #10 – SPAM Prevention

Everybody hates comment spam. Fortunately, the All in One plugin includes a few features to help combat comment spam.

Click on the **SPAM Prevention** menu.

There are three tabs across the top.

The first one is the **Comment Spam** settings.

One way to cut down on spam comments is to add a Captcha to the comment form. Captchas don't stop spammers leaving comments, though. But they do make life more difficult and inconvenient for them, and that's a good thing. The **Add Captcha to Comments Form** options is a "Basic" feature, so it's safe to implement right away. For this, you'll get 20 more points towards your security score.

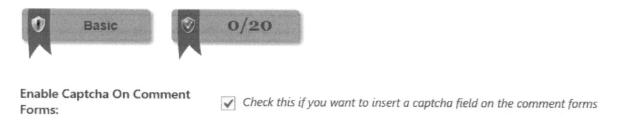

**Enable Captcha On Comment Forms:** ✓ *Check this if you want to insert a captcha field on the comment forms*

Once saved, your comment form will have something like this above the **Post Comment** button:

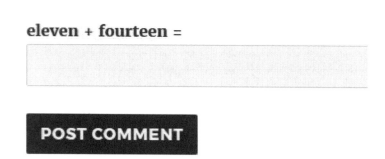

PLEASE ENTER AN ANSWER IN DIGITS:

**eleven + fourteen =**

POST COMMENT

This means a human will need to enter the answer for the comment to arrive in your pending list.

Also on the **Comment Spam** settings is the option to **Block Spambots from Posting Comments**. Spambots are pieces of software that allow mass submission of comments to hundreds or thousands of sites in a very short space of time. This plugin can tell if it's a spambot trying to post because, unlike a real visitor, the request to post a comment won't originate from your domain. We can, therefore, block spambots from posting by checking the **Block Spambots from Posting Comments** checkbox.

Save settings before continuing.

The second tab on the **SPAM Prevention** settings is the **Comment SPAM IP Monitoring** settings.

When spam comments get into your site, you can approve them, send them to trash, or mark them as spam (get familiar with spam comments).

The Spam option is the one you should use. Together with this plugin, comments marked as spam can trigger an automatic block on the IP that posted it.

Here are the settings I recommend:

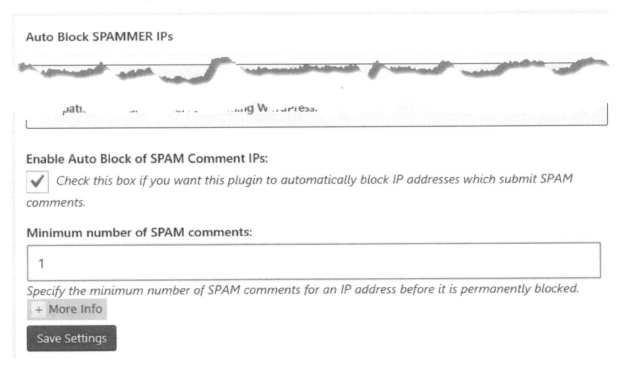

Whenever you mark a comment as spam in the future, the plugin will add the IP address of the sender to the blocked IP list. The reason I choose 1 for the "minimum number of spam comments" is simple. If someone sends me even one spam comment, I want them blocked.

All the IP addresses of blocked Spam comments will now appear further down this screen in the **Spammer IP Address Results** table.

Save your settings before moving on.

The final tab on the Spam Prevention settings is only available for those using BuddyPress. If BuddyPress is running, this option can add a Captcha to the BuddyPress registration form. Since I don't have BuddyPress running, there's nothing to see here.

# Setting #11 – Scanner

When a hacker breaks into your site, they'll usually change one or more files on your server. A typical hack would involve injecting malicious code into these files. If successful, they can then use your site for their evil purposes.

Auto email notifications are a great way to catch hackers early on if any files on your server change unexpectedly. In general, WordPress core files, plugin files, and theme files don't change too often. PHP files and JavaScript files are the prime targets of most hackers.

Our plugin can monitor these files and notify you right away if something changes. You'll obviously know if it was you who made the changes the last time you were in your Dashboard. If not, it'll be something or someone more sinister.

The first step to monitoring files is to carry out an initial scan. The plugin can then compare files in the future based on the scan date. At the top of the options screen, click **Perform Scan Now** in the **Manual File Change Detection Scan**.

Under the manual scan is a button that allows you to see files that have changed since the last scan. There won't be anything to see yet as we're just setting it up.

The next panel on this screen is the real workhorse. It carries out automated checks at predefined intervals. This is an "Intermediate" feature, though. Only activate it once you know your basic protection is working fine.

When you're ready, check the **Enable Automated File Change Detection Scan** box.

The default scan frequency is four weeks. The interval you choose determines how long hackers have before the system notifies you. A scan interval of four weeks means it could be four weeks before you find out about any changes.

Note that these scans do take up server resources. Therefore, don't do anything like scan every hour. That's UNLESS you think a hacker is attempting to break into your site and you want to monitor the situation.

I tend to stick to a 2 – 4-week scan interval on my own sites.

You can also set the scan up to ignore certain file types. For example, if you post a lot of images, it's wise to ignore the image file formats you use:

File Types To Ignore:

jpg
png

You can get the scan to ignore files or directories as well. If you know where your log files are, or their names, you can exclude those. Similarly, you might want to ignore any caching folder if these are just cached copies of your web pages.

Enter the address you want to use for auto email notifications at the bottom of the screen. Click **Save Changes**.

The **Malware Scan** tab is information about malware and links to tools you can use to scan for malware on your site. There are no settings on this screen.

# Setting #12 – Maintenance

When you want to lock visitors out of your site for any length of time, you can put your site into **Maintenance Mode**. We touched on this earlier when we first looked at the plugin's Dashboard.

The **Maintenance** screen gives you some **Visitor Lockout options.**

The **Enable Front-End Lockout** checkbox will turn maintenance mode on. Visitors will see a message to say that your site is not live right now. The content of the **Enter a Message** box determines the exact message.

The default message simply states the site is not available and to try again later. You can change this message to read whatever you like. The editor for this is a full WYSIWYG, so you can control the format, and even include images, and links, etc.

If you do change the default message, make sure you save the settings before proceeding. Also, make sure you have **Enable Font-end Lockout** DISABLED unless you actually want it enabled right now.

# Setting #13 - Miscellaneous

The final settings for this plugin are grouped together in the **Miscellaneous** screen.

Here there are three tabs.

The first one is the **Copy Protection tab**. This prevents people from right clicking on your web pages. It's useful because they can't get the right click popup menu to inspect (and steal) your web page content. It also stops people from highlighting blocks of text on your page, so makes copying your content more difficult.

This feature won't stop a determined hacker. It will certainly deter some common thieves, though, who simply want to steal your content.

Check the **Enable Copy Protection** box, and save the settings.

On the **Frames** tab, there are options to stop other people putting your web pages in a frame on their own websites. This type of technique allows them to trick visitors into thinking they're actually on your site. Needless to say, this is a practice that can be quite damaging to you.

To prevent this, check the **Enable iFrame Protection** box, and save settings.

The **Users Enumeration** tab has one option. **Disable Users Enumeration** will prevent hackers (or bots) from accessing useful "hacking info."

Check the box and save the settings.

OK, that's the plugin all set up. Your site is now really well-protected.

Go back and check your Security score. Your results will depend on which features you have activated. Here's how mine looks now:

I've achieved this score after activating some "Intermediate" and "Advanced" features. Don't worry right now if your score's a lot less. It'll increase as you go in and activate more features over time.

I still have a few other features to activate on my site, so my score will go up a little more from what it is.

Notice the above image on the right. When we first began to activate the plugin, that pie chart looked like the one below:

I'm feeling a lot more confident now that my site is secure.

In reality, though, no site is ever 100% safe against the most determined hackers. You probably know this already after seeing the successful hacks of high profile internet companies. However, the measures you've taken here will keep your site safe against 99.9% of hackers. The ones who could succeed are likely to be more interested in much bigger, higher profile prey.

And remember, even if the worst did happen — including a server meltdown and your web host not having a backup — it's not the end of the world. You have all the necessary files to restore your own site with the backups you've done (and automated) as you went through this book.

In the next chapter, I provide you with a security checklist. This will help you to methodically work your way through as you protect your website(s).

Remember, start with the "**Basic**" features first. Test them for a while before activating some "**Intermediate**" features. Test again for a while, and then go in and tweak some of the "Advanced" options.

# Chapter 11 - Security Checklist

This checklist includes items of all the main security fixes you should carry out on your WordPress website. I've included a complete list of those I enable on my own sites. If there're any in this list you don't want to implement, just skip them.

The sub-headings refer to the section of the WP security plugin you have to visit to carry out the steps. Some screens have tabs. If I tell you to go to a specific tab, you'll always find it along the top of the screen.

Before you begin to setup the security on a new site, I recommend you scan your site first and do a few backups.

If you want to download this list as a PDF, I have created one you can grab from here:

http://ezseonews.com/securelist

## Initial Tests and Backups

### 1. Not Included in the Plugin

☐ Disable PHP error reporting

### 2. Scanner Menu

☐ On the **File Change Detection** tab, **Perform Scan Now** to check if any files are different from the default installation files. You may find that the .htaccess file has changed, but that's usually fine.

☐ Check the option to **Enable Automated File Change Detection Scan**.

### 3. Settings Menu

☐ Backup your Database
☐ Backup your .htaccess file
☐ Backup your wp-config.php
☐ Click on the **WP version Info** tab across the top and check the **Remove WP Generator Meta** box.

## Setting up Security

### User Accounts Menu

☐ On the **WP** Username tab, ensure you are not using **admin** as username.
☐ On the **Display Name** tab, ensure your login name and display name are different.

## User Login Menu

- ☐ On the **Login Lockdown** tab, enable **Login Lockdown.**
- ☐ On the **Force Logout** tab, enable the **Force WP User Logout.**

## User Registration Menu

- ☐ On the **Manual Approval** tab, enable **Manual approval of new registrations.**
- ☐ On the **Registration Captcha** tab, enable **Captcha on Registration Page.**

## Database Security

- ☐ On the **DB Prefix** tab, make sure you're not using the default wp_ as your table prefix.
- ☐ On the **DB Backup** tab, enable automated backups.

## Filesystem Security

- ☐ On the **File Permissions** tab, if there are any **Recommended Actions**, take them.
- ☐ On the **PHP File Editing** tab, **Disable ability to edit PHP Files.**
- ☐ On the **WP File Access** tab, **Prevent Access to WP Default Install Files.**

## Firewall

- ☐ On the **Basic Firewall Rules** tab, **Enable Basic Firewall Protection.**
- ☐ If you are not using XMLRPC, you can block it completely; however, I don't recommend this as some plugins will use it.
- ☐ Enable the **Block Access to debug.log file.**
- ☐ On the **Additional Firewall Rules** tab, enable **Disable Index Views.**
- ☐ Enable the **Disable Trace and Track.**
- ☐ Enable **Forbid Proxy Comment Posting.**
- ☐ Enable **Deny Bad Query Strings.**
- ☐ Enable the **Enable Advanced Character String Filter.**
- ☐ On the **6G Blacklist Firewall Rules** tab, check the **Enable 6G Firewall Protection** option.
- ☐ On the **Internet Bots** tab, enable the option to **Block Fake Googlebots.**
- ☐ On the **Prevent Hotlinks** tab, enable the option to **Prevent Image Hotlinking.**
- ☐ On the **404 Detection** tab, check the option to **Enable 404 IP Detection and Lockout.**

## Brute Force

- ☐ On the **Cookie Based Brute Force Prevention**, perform the cookie test to make sure your site can use this method of protection. If it can, enter a **Secret** Word and then **Enable Brute Force Attack Prevention** on this tab. If it cannot, go to the **Rename Login Page** tab and use that instead.

☐ On the **Login Captcha** tab, enable any of the captchas that you want to use.

☐ On the **Honeypot** tab, check the option to **Enable Honeypot on Login Page**.

## SPAM Prevention

☐ On the **Comment Spam** tab, check the option to **Enable Captcha On Comment Forms**.

☐ Check the option to **Block Spambots from posting comments**.

☐ On the **Comment SPAM IP Monitoring** tab, check the option to **Enable Auto Block of SPAM Comment IPs**. I recommend you enter a low number into the **Minimum number of SPAM comments** box. I use 1.

## Miscellaneous

☐ On the **Copy Protection** tab, check the option to **Enable Copy Protection**.

☐ On the **Frames** tab, check the option to **Enable iFrame Protection**.

☐ On the **Users Enumeration** tab, check the option to **Disable Users Enumeration**.

# Chapter 12 - Further Reading

I've included a list of recommended reading for anyone who's interested in learning more about website security.

I have duplicated the list with clickable links here if you want to view this list in your web browser: http://ezseonews.com/securitylinks


https://www.wordfence.com/learn/introduction-to-WordPress-security/

http://makeawebsitehub.com/WordPress-security/

https://premium.wpmudev.org/blog/keeping-WordPress-secure-the-ultimate-guide/

https://yoast.com/WordPress-security/

http://www.tripwire.com/state-of-security/featured/5-best-WordPress-security-plugins-to-keep-your-site-secure/

# Where to Go from Here?

We've covered a lot of ground in this book. You should now be confident finding your way around the WordPress Dashboard.

You've installed WordPress, installed the essential plugins, and configured everything so that your site is now ready for content.

So, what's the next step?

**Create impressive content!**

Everything we've done in this book has been to achieve one main goal. Get your site set up & ready to accept your content. You can now concentrate on publishing your pages while WordPress takes care of the rest.

Here is your simple plan going forward.

1. Create a post.
2. Publish it.
3. Rinse and repeat steps 1 and 2.

If you want a "static" homepage — rather than one that shows the most recent posts — then create a PAGE with the content you want to display. Then set the **reading** settings so the content shows permanently on your site's home page. You can then go back to the 3-step process outlined above

Create a post, publish & repeat. That's it!

Good luck!

Andy Williams

http://ezSEONews.com

# My Resources

There are a few places I recommend you visit for more information.

## My ezSEONews Website

http://ezSEONews.com – This is my site where I offer free help and advice to webmasters. While you're there, sign up for my free weekly newsletter. You can also look through past issues and read articles on a variety of topics related to building WordPress sites.

## My Other Webmaster Books

All my books are available as Kindle eBooks and paperbacks. View them here:

http://amazon.com/author/drandrewwilliams

I'll leave you to explore those if you're interested. You'll find books on various aspects of being a webmaster such as creating high-quality content, SEO, CSS, etc.

## My Video Courses

I have a growing number of video courses hosted on Udemy. You can view a complete list of these at my site:

http://ezseonews.com/udemy

There are courses on the same kinds of topics that my books cover, so SEO, Content Creation, WordPress, Website Analytics, and so on.

# Please Leave a Review/Thought on Amazon

If you enjoyed this book, or even if you didn't, I'd love to hear your comments about it. You can leave your thoughts on the Amazon website.

Printed in Great Britain
by Amazon